The Bodybuilding Prep Cookbook

Complete Step By Step Guide To Cooking The Best Bodybuilding Recipes And Getting Your Best Muscles Ever With The 6 Week Diet Plan For Men And Women

Introduction

Have you ever wondered what professional bodybuilders do to get that chiseled physique apart from spending time at the gym, and your research has revealed that diet is the other key ingredient for a well-toned, chiseled look?

And, would you like to know what it takes to feed your muscles for bulking up, so you can effectively build muscle and lift more while enjoying flavorful and delicious meals?

Well then, if this is so, your answers are in this book so continue reading…

You are about to learn how to create finger-licking dishes at the comfort of your kitchen to help you build up a perfect physique using quick and easy to follow bodybuilding recipes!

Without discipline and following a working plan, maintaining a toned physique and bulking up cannot be accomplished easily.

By now, you probably know the exercise regimens that best suit you- but do you know that the food you eat and how you prepare your meals also affects how much you can bulk?

Yes, without eating the right foods, you might end up damaging your muscles instead of building them!

Don't worry though, if you do not have any idea of where to get started, as this definitive guide will walk you through all the steps you'll need to take to help you achieve the body you've been dreaming of for so long.

The fact that you are here means you are already looking to optimize your diet so that you can get the most out of it for that toned, chiseled look you have in your mind.

Perhaps you are wondering...

What foods should I eat when bodybuilding?

Are there foods that I should not eat?

How does the food I eat affect muscle growth?

How much food should I be eating?

How do I turn bodybuilding foods into delicious meals?

How do I fit my meals into a 6-week diet plan and beyond?

If you have these and other related questions, then this book has everything you need to get started with meal prepping for bodybuilding and prepare hassle-free and quick dishes.

Here is a preview of what you'll learn in this cookbook:

- The proper nutrients to include when preparing bodybuilding meals

- **The pillars of a fat burning/muscle building diet**

- A 6-week bodybuilding nutrition program to make it easier for you to create meals that move you closer to your target look and body fat/muscle composition

- **Mouth-watering recipes for your breakfasts, dinner, lunch, and snacks to get you started**

- And much more....

Whether you want to shed off excess weight, maintain your body physique, or build up muscle, this cookbook will help you hit your daily macro goals with a collection of delicious and easy to prep recipes.

Let's get started!

Table of Contents

Introduction _____ 2

Chapter 1: Pillars Of The Bulking Diet ____ 11

    How To Build Muscle Through Diet _____ 11

    How Muscles Grow _____ 12

    How To Create A Working Muscle Building Diet 13

    Bodybuilding Macros _____ 14

    Meal Prepping For Muscle Gain _____ 18

    Why It Is Important To Meal Prep _____ 23

Chapter 2: Bodybuilding Recipes _____ 25

Breakfast Recipes _____ 25

    Vegetable Egg White Frittata Recipe _____ 25

    Fruit and Yogurt Parfaits _____ 29

    Pina Colada Instant Pot Steel Cut Oats _____ 32

    Breakfast Taco Scramble_____ 34

    Crockpot Breakfast Casserole_____ 38

Quinoa Breakfast Meal Prep 41

Banana Egg Pancakes 44

Sweet Potato Breakfast Bowls 46

Sheet Tray Pancakes 49

High Protein Salmon Toast 52

Protein Waffles 54

Baked Omelet Muffins 56

Protein Pancakes 59

Egg Muffins with Cauliflower Rice, Ham, and Kale 62

Bacon-Wrapped Egg Cups 65

Egg and Sausage McMuffin 67

Peanut Butter Protein Pancakes 70

Overnight Oats 73

Tex Mex Breakfast Quesadillas 80

Salmon Eggs Benedict with Avocado Hollandaise 83

Vegan Freezer Breakfast Burritos 86

Protein-Packed Breakfast Burritos _____ 89

Vegetarian Black Bean Breakfast Burritos _____ 91

Egg and Avocado Breakfast _____ 96

Simple Toast With Avocado And Poached Egg 99

Main Meal Recipes _____ 102

Simple Turkey Chili _____ 102

Chicken Taco Soup _____ 105

Kung Pao Chicken _____ 108

Avocado Chicken Salad _____ 112

Light Mongolian Beef _____ 114

Greek Marinated Chicken _____ 117

Jerk Chicken Bowls _____ 120

Creamy Spinach Chicken with Zucchini Noodles _____ 122

Chickpea Quinoa Salad _____ 126

General Tso's Chickpeas _____ 129

Chicken And Avocado Burritos _____ 134

Spicy Chicken and Sweet Potato _____ 136

Healthy Cashew Chicken Casserole _____ 139

Korean Turkey Meal Prep Bowls _____ 142

Roasted Brussels Sprout Bowls _____ 146

Steak Cobb Salad Meal Prep _____ 150

Salsa Chicken Bowls _____ 153

Cashew Chicken Sheet Pan _____ 157

Maple Ginger Chicken Lunch Bowls _____ 161

Quinoa And Steak Burrito Bowl _____ 164

Hummus Lunch Box _____ 168

Egg Roll in a Bowl _____ 170

Chicken Salad with Creamy No-Mayo Dressing 173

The Pizza Roll-Up Lunch Box _____ 177

Tuna Salad _____ 180

Cold Sesame Noodles Made With Spiralized Vegetables _____ 183

Smoky Roasted Sausage And Vegetables _____ 186

Sheet Pan ginger, Garlic Chicken and Broccoli 190

Buddha Bowl 193

Honey Sesame Chicken Bowls 196

Honey Sriracha Glazed Meatballs 200

Cheesy Chicken and Rice 203

Snacks Recipes 206

Quinoa Peanut Butter Cup Protein Balls 209

Peanut Butter Bites 211

No-Bake Pb & J Energy Bites 214

Protein Brownie Bites 217

Healthy Chocolate Raspberry Protein Bars 220

Apple Pie Protein Bars 222

Sweet Pumpkin Protein Granola 225

Chocolate Chip Raspberry Crispy Granola Bars 229

Carrot Cake Power Bites 232

Vanilla Cashew Butter Cups 236

14 Day Meal Plan 239

Week 1 Meal Plan — 239

- Day 1 — 239
- Day 2 — 239
- Day 3 — 240
- Day 4 — 240
- Day 5 — 241
- Day 6 — 241
- Day 7 — 242

Week Two Meal Plan — 243

- Day 8 — 243
- Day 9 — 243
- Day 10 — 244
- Day 11 — 244
- Day 12 — 245
- Day 13 — 245
- Day 14 — 246

Conclusion — 247

Before we get to the specifics of bodybuilding, especially regarding the recipes you can prepare to achieve that, you must build your understanding of what it takes to bulk up through diet. That's why this will be our first chapter.

Chapter 1: Pillars Of The Bulking Diet

If you've been struggling with sticking to your daily calorie goals and gaining muscle mass despite following your workout regime to the letter, it is probably because you are not eating the right foods to fuel muscle growth or your diet is not well organized.

Just as following a bodybuilding regimen can be difficult, preparing a meal plan can be similarly daunting. Meal prep is an effective way of keeping your diet organized, keeping yourself accountable, and delivering consistently – which helps you attain perfect results, within a consistently short time.

How To Build Muscle Through Diet

To bulk up, you'll need to increase your calorie intake. However, a few factors will determine whether the weight you gain is fat or muscle – including your lifestyle, your specific workout routine, and the type of foods you eat.

You should keep in mind that to gain muscle, you'll also be gaining some fat – and the amount of fat you gain may vary from one person to another.

So, how do you deal with potential weight gain and tip the odds more in your favor for muscle gain?

Well, with the right approach and mindset, it quite easy. However, to get a clearer picture, we'll first need to understand how muscle growth works.

How Muscles Grow

When working out, you challenge your muscles to counter higher weight or resistance levels. This causes damage to your muscles. Although it might seem like a counterintuitive thing to do, in essence, it what needs to be done to build muscle mass.

So, how does the damage lead to muscle mass?

The damage caused to muscle, known as microtears, causes your body to respond by sending more blood and nutrients to the affected areas for the healing process. The damaged muscle fibers are then repaired or replaced through a cellular process whereby the muscle fibers are fused together, hence forming new myofibrils (new muscle strands). This increases the number and thickness of the myofibrils – leading to muscle growth (hypertrophy).

However, this process does not happen when you are working out but rather as you rest. So, in essence, optimal muscle building is about exerting your muscles enough to cause the right amount of muscle tears, giving the body time to recover, and providing it with the right nutrients to aid in the recovery process in a way that ensures muscle repair and subsequent growth.

This book focuses primarily on the diet part. Let's look at the best meal prep strategy that revolves around the foods and recipes that can meet your fitness and nutrition needs.

How To Create A Working Muscle Building Diet

To create a diet that will allow you to hit your daily macro and calorie intake goals, you'll need to ensure that it is comprised of foods that you enjoy eating and foods that allow you to hit your daily intake goals. Moreover, to support muscle growth, you'll need to go for more nutritious options as opposed to empty calories. To achieve this, we'll need to focus on macros, which are the main pillars of the bulking diet.

Let's take a look.

Bodybuilding Macros

The most effective way of balancing your calories and nutrition in one take is by understanding how to count your daily macros.

So, what are macros?

"Macro" is a shortened version of the word macronutrients, which are the sources of calories. There are different types of macros, and each one impacts muscle growth differently. The three main types of macros to focus on when bodybuilding include; fat, carbohydrates, and protein.

Let's take a look at each one of them in detail:

Proteins

This is one of the most important macros for gaining muscle mass, as it is the primary building block for all muscle tissues. Protein is mainly comprised of amino acids, which cause and aid most of the processes and reactions in your body.

When you eat proteins after a workout, your body breaks them down and uses the amino acids to aid in repairing the damage to muscle tissue by surrounding and filling the microtears. This, therefore, means that your diet will have to be high in proteins to increase your lean mass and enhance muscle growth.

So, how much protein do you need to eat to build muscle?

Basically, the average recommendation for bodybuilders is 1.2 to 1.7 grams of protein for every kilogram of body weight per day. For instance, if you weigh 70 kilograms (154 pounds), you should eat between 84 and 119 grams of protein per day. However, the amount of protein you consume will also be dependent on other factors, including gender, height, and level of activity.

When adding proteins to your diet, you should keep in mind that per 1 gram, they provide 4 calories. Research done recommends that you should ensure that proteins comprise approximately 10-35% of your total calorie intake.

Some examples of protein-rich foods to add to your diet include; eggs, fish, lentils, tofu, beef, turkey, cottage cheese, beans, lentils, mixed nuts, and peanut butter.

Carbohydrates

Carbs provide the body with energy; hence they are an important addition to your bodybuilding diet as they can support muscle recovery and help you fuel your body when working out.

Your body breaks carbohydrates into blood sugar (glucose), which it uses for instant energy. If there is any excess glucose, the liver converts the excess into glycogen, which is then stored in your muscles and liver for later use.

As a plus, carbs also trigger an insulin response that helps support weight/muscle gain – when glycogen stores are filled up, any excess glucose is converted into fatty acids and glycerol, which ultimately causes weight gain. This, therefore, means that consuming more carbs will support your increased calorie requirements when working out.

Carbs usually include fibers, sugars, and starches. For every gram of carbs, you get 4 calories. Research shows that you should consume at least 45-65% of your total calories from carbs.

Carbs can be found in foods such as beans, grains, fruits, dairy products, and starchy vegetables.

Fats:

These provide the body with energy for longer as compared to carbs, which provide you with short and quick bursts of energy. Fats provide the body with twice as many calories per

1 gram, as compared to the other macros going up to 9 calories per gram.

Dietary fat plays a key role in the production of vital hormones that stimulate fat burning and promote muscle growth. It also helps your body synthesize protein and absorb fat-soluble nutrients.

The downside to consuming too much fat is that it can cause increased fat storage if your body has a calorie surplus. This is why it is advisable to add moderate amounts of fat to your bodybuilding diet and consume more calories from proteins and carbs (20-35% of your total calories).

You can add foods such as fatty fish, nuts, oils, meat, nuts, avocado, and butter to your bodybuilding diet for healthy fats.

You can rely on [this calculator](#) to determine the specific amount you need for each macronutrient.

Now that you know your macro and calorie goals, along with some of the best foods that you should add to your bodybuilding meal prep routine, we can now take a look at how you can curate the most effective meal plan that is focused on muscle gain.

Meal Prepping For Muscle Gain

Meal prep involves planning and prepping your meals in advance. To do this, you should start by selecting one day of the week that you'd like to prepare and cook the foods.

Most people prefer Saturdays and Sundays for meal prepping.

Below are the steps to help you create a weekly meal prep.

Step 1: Plan your menu and timing your meals

Understanding the specific foods that you should be eating and at what time of the day is an essential factor to consider if you want to succeed in bodybuilding, regardless of whether you are a woman or a man.

The reason why this is important is that:

1. It helps you spread out your daily intake of protein throughout the day, which helps you absorb a higher amount of the protein you eat.

2. It allows you to get sufficient amounts of calories throughout the day by eating small and frequent meals

3. It helps you get more out of your recovery and workouts by allowing you to have post and pre-workout meals.

To be sure that your prep sets you up for success, it is important to come up with a menu for a whole week upfront. You can tweak the menu to suit each day's workout and set appropriate times for the meals throughout the day.

Below are some tips to make your meal prep more effective:

1. Use recipes that provide you with the relevant macro information that can help you come up with a menu based on your nutrition needs (provided in this book).

2. Create a weekly calendar and write all meals for each day (also provided later in the book). You can also include the time of the day that you'll be working out.

3. Note down all the ingredients you need to prepare all the recipes for each week and create a shopping list based on that

4. Don't forget to add desserts, snacks, and beverages to your menu! You can even go ahead a schedule one cheat meal per week

Post And Pre-Workout Meals

When coming up with your weekly menu, you need to factor in the calorie requirement difference between working out days and rest days. You can make up for this difference by adding more meals or small snacks around the training window.

You should aim to get a meal a few hours before working out – ensuring that you include a healthy and balanced meal that contains sufficient amounts of protein and plenty of carbs. If you usually workout after waking up or you simply need to add a snack before hitting the gym, you should consider eating simple sugars or quick-acting carbs such as a small muffin, chocolate milk, or a sports drink to help you fuel your workout session.

After your workouts, you'll need to consume sufficient amounts of protein, quick carbs, and moderate amounts of fat to allow for quicker absorption. At this stage, you can consider trying protein shakes, chicken and white rice, fruit, cottage cheese, or chocolate milk.

Step 2: Cooking your meals

Cooking is a vital part of meal prep that you simply can't avoid (unless you prefer to get your meals from a meal prep delivery company!). Below are some tips to help you get the most out of your kitchen.

1. If you do not consider yourself a good cook, then you should set realistic goals and go for recipes that you feel you can execute comfortably. You don't want to be feeling like cooking is a burden and end up giving up on your bodybuilding diet. Remember that you'll be spending more time in the kitchen preparing food for the week.

2. Cook in batches to help you reduce the amount of time you spend in the kitchen. You try preparing large one-pot meals such as pilafs, lasagna, chili, or any other recipe that can be cooked in bulk, then split throughout the week.

3. Cook foods that are related once and use different sauces and seasonings to change the flavors. For instance, add all your veggies and proteins to one sheet pan, coat them with different seasonings and cook them together.

4. Repeat simple side dishes such as salad, rice, and sweet potatoes for multiple meals

Step 3: Reheating your meals

Another part of meal prepping in advance involves cooking foods that can work well for reheating and as leftovers. Some meals are great for this, while others simply do not cut it. Below are some other tips that you should consider before you cook:

1. Ensure that you go for a meal prep container that best suits your unique needs such as the size of your potions, how easy they are to clean and travel with, and if they are dishwasher safe, or if they can be used in an oven or microwave.

2. You also need to consider the options you have for reheating if it's an option and the location you'll be eating your food & the reheating options in the specific location.

3. Consider if you'll need to travel with your food and the methods that you'll employ to keep it fresh and cold.

To reheat your food and make it feel less like leftover food, there a few things you can try out, including;

1. Warming your food on a stovetop or in an oven, if possible, to ensure that your proteins do not dry out and your vegetables remain crispy and nice.

2. After warming the food and you are ready to dig in, you can add some finishing salt to liven the flavors

3. Sprinkle citrus or some fresh herbs on top of the food after reheating

4. Pack your garnishes and sauces on the side

Step 4: Tracking your intake and portioning your food

It is recommended that you use a food tracking app to track your daily intake. This way, you'll be able to get a more accurate calculation of the number of calories and macros that you consume every day.

You'll also be able to see an estimate of the calories and macros that you consume each week. However, you should not forget to account for the unexpected foods that might find their way into your diet, including your cheat meal.

Using precise food portions is an effective way of ensuring that you accurately track your intake. You should consider using measuring spoons or cups or getting a food scale to weigh your protein potions when you cook to help you consider the number of calories in your ingredients.

Why It Is Important To Meal Prep

- *It makes healthy eating effortless:* Meal prepping helps make it a lot easier for you to make healthy eating decisions. If you plan ahead, you won't have to spend time thinking about what to cook for a couple of days – meaning you won't opt to go for takeout on those lazy days!

- *Your food is Pre-portioned:* When building muscle and losing fat, it is vital to fuel your body with the correct amounts of nutrients and calories. This means that if you don't meal prep, you'll have to keep weighing your food daily to get your calories right – which can be confusing, tiresome, and awkward. Meal prepping eliminates this problem and allows you to pre-portion and pre-pack your meals, enabling you to support your fitness goal.

- *Allows you time your nutrients:* As stated earlier, to get the best out of your bodybuilding training, it is important to eat enough carbs and proteins at the appropriate times of the day to allow muscle growth and recovery and stop muscle breakdown (catabolism). Meal prepping allows you to make it easier for you to eat the food that is required by your body and at the proper times of the day. For instance, when meal prepping, you can decide what to eat before workouts and after workouts in advance.

Chapter 2: Bodybuilding Recipes

Now that you know what it takes to meal prep for bodybuilding, you can now prepare yourself to whip up delicious meals in your kitchen using the recipes outlined in this chapter – which are easy to cook and have well-balanced macros to ensure that you get the best out of bodybuilding.

Each of the recipes listed has high protein and uses simple ingredients that will make it easy for you, even if you've never cooked before.

Let's dive in!

Breakfast Recipes

Vegetable Egg White Frittata Recipe

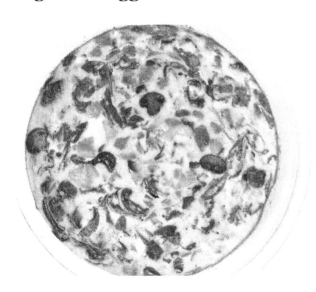

Prep time: 5 minutes

Cook time: 45 minutes

Total time: 50 minutes

Servings: 4

Ingredients

32 oz of liquid egg whites

1/3 cup of diced bell pepper

1/3 cup of diced cherry tomatoes

1 to 2 tablespoons of olive oil

1 teaspoon of onion powder

½ teaspoon of paprika

1 cup of cottage cheese

2 cups of spinach

1/3 cup of mushrooms

1 teaspoon of turmeric powder

½ teaspoon of garlic powder

1 teaspoon of salt

Directions

1. Preheat your oven to 350 degrees. Warm a 9-inch casserole dish inside the oven before you cook

2. Over medium-high heal, use a skillet to warm oil

3. Add the spinach, then turn off the heat

4. Add the cottage cheese and egg whites to a blender and pulse on a high setting until your mixture is thoroughly combined.

5. Take out the casserole dish from the oven and add the vegetables to it. Ensure you spread them out evenly.

6. Pour the 9-inch egg mixture you made over the vegetables in the casserole dish.

7. Cook for about 45 minutes to 1 hour, or until the center has cooked through. Remove and allow it to cool for about 15 minutes before you serve.

8. Enjoy!

Nutritional information: Calories 140, Fat3g, Protein 23g, Carbs 5g

Recipe notes

Store the frittata in an airtight container until you are ready to eat. To reheat, you can either use the oven at 300 degrees for 5-10 minutes or in a microwave for 1 ½ minute

Fruit and Yogurt Parfaits

Prep time: 10 minutes

Cook time: 0 minutes

Total time: 10 minutes

Servings: 1

Ingredients

1/2 cup mixed berries (strawberries, blueberries, raspberries)

1 tablespoon of granola

3/4 cup of Greek yogurt (or dairy-free yogurt, plain yogurt)

1 teaspoon of maple syrup

1/2 tablespoon of coconut flakes (optional)

Directions

1. Start by washing the berries. If some of them are too big, then chop them into smaller pieces
2. To a mason jar, add 2-3 tablespoons of yogurt.
3. Add half of the fruits you chopped.
4. Add the yogurt that remained.
5. Top it with the remaining mixed berries, coconut flakes, maple syrup, and granola.
6. Fasten the mason jar lid and store it in your refrigerator for up to 3-4 days.
7. When you are ready to eat, you should simply remove it from the fridge, mix it and enjoy.

Nutritional information: Calories 210, Fat 5g, Protein 17g, Carbs 27g

Recipe notes

1. The yogurt parfaits can be stored in the refrigerator for up to 4 days in an airtight container or a mason jar.

2. If you prefer eating crunchy granola, you should consider adding it the night before the morning you are going to eat your yogurt. However, if you do not mind eating soft granola, you should add it when meal prepping.

Pina Colada Instant Pot Steel Cut Oats

Prep time: 10 minutes

Cook time: 35 minutes

Total time: 45 minutes

Servings: 4

Ingredients

1 tablespoon of coconut oil

2 cups of coconut milk (from a carton)

1 cup of water

1 cup of steel-cut oats

1 1/2 cups of fresh & diced pineapple

3/4 cup of sweetened shredded coconut

Cherries or Raspberries for topping (optional)

Directions

1. In an instant pot, pour the coconut oil, coconut milk, water, and steel-cut oats in that exact order. Cook for about 3 minutes on high pressure, then let the pressure release naturally, for about 20-25 minutes.

2. When the pressure is fully released, the lid will open easily. Remove it and stir in the pineapple and shredded coconut. Divide the meal into 4 meal prep bowls and garnish with cherries and raspberries (optional).

3. Serve and enjoy!

Nutritional information: Calories 233, Fat 13g, Protein 4g, Carbs 28g

Breakfast Taco Scramble

Prep time:10 minutes

Cook time:50 minutes

Total time: 1 hour

Servings: 4

Ingredients

1/4 teaspoon of adobo seasoning salt

1 lb. of 99% lean turkey, ground

1/2 small onion, minced

4 oz can of tomato sauce

1/4 cup of chopped cilantro or scallions, for the topping

8 large eggs, beaten

1/2 cup of reduced-fat shredded cheese (Mexican blend)

2 tablespoons of taco seasoning (see below for homemade version)

2 tablespoons of bell pepper, minced

1/4 cup of water

salsa, for serving

For the potatoes:

4 teaspoons of olive oil

1/2 teaspoon of garlic powder

12 1 lb. of res or baby gold potatoes, quartered

3/4 teaspoon of salt

fresh black pepper, to taste

For homemade taco seasoning:

1 teaspoon of garlic powder

1 teaspoon of kosher salt, or to taste

1 teaspoon of paprika

1 teaspoon of cumin

1 teaspoon of chili powder

1/2 teaspoon of oregano

Directions

1. Beat the eggs in a large bowl and season with salt. Add the cheese.

2. Preheat your oven to 425F. Meanwhile, spray a large oval or 9x12 casserole dish with oil.

3. Add in the black pepper, garlic powder, ¾ tablespoon of salt, potatoes, and 1 tablespoon of oil, then toss.

4. Bake until tender as you toss every 15 minutes. Repeat this for about 45 minutes to 1 hour.

5. Meanwhile, use a large skillet to brown the turkey in over medium heat, breaking up as it cooks. When it is no longer pink, add in the spices and mix thoroughly.

6. Add the water, tomato sauce, onion, and bell pepper, then stir and cover it up. Let it simmer on low heat for around 20 minutes.

7. Use a non-stick spray to spray another skillet, then add the ¼ teaspoon of salt and eggs, then scramble. Let it cook until just set, for approximately 2-3 minutes.

8. To serve for meal prep, place 2/3 cup eggs and ¾ cup of turkey in each bowl or plate, then divide the potatoes and top each of the servings with cilantro or scallions, 1 tablespoon of cheese, and salsa on the side.

Nutritional information: Calories 450, Fat 19g, Protein 46g, Carbs 24.5g

Crockpot Breakfast Casserole

Prep time: 20 minutes

Cook time: 4 hours

Total time: 4 hours 20 minutes

Servings: 8

Ingredients

2 cups of frozen hash browns

1 yellow, 1 red, and 1 green bell pepper, diced

16 large eggs

1/2 teaspoon of pepper

Cooking spray

12 slices of turkey or pork bacon

1 medium-sized diced red onion

1 teaspoon of salt

1 cup of grated cheddar cheese

Directions

1. In a large skillet, cook the bacon over medium-high heat for approximately 5-10 minutes or until cooked through (the time is dependent on the type of bacon you choose).

2. Use a cooking spray to spray the inside of a slow cooker, then add cooked bacon, onions, peppers, and the frozen hash browns in 2 even layers. Meanwhile, mix the pepper and salt with the eggs, then pour the mixture over the layers and top it with cheese.

3. Cook on high heat for approximately 4 hours.

4. Serve and enjoy!

Nutritional information: Calories 486, Fat 34g, Protein 31g, Carbs 14g

Recipe notes

1. This meal can be made 3 days in advance for meal prep.

Quinoa Breakfast Meal Prep

Prep time: 5 minutes

Cook time: 15 minutes

Total time: 20 minutes

Servings: 4

Ingredients

2 cups of almond milk

1/4 teaspoon of ground cardamom

4 cups of mixed berries

1 cup of quinoa

1/2 teaspoon of ground cinnamon

2 tablespoons of maple syrup

4 tablespoons of sliced almonds

Directions

1. Combine the cardamom, cinnamon, quinoa, and almond milk in a medium-sized pot.

2. Bring it to boil, then reduce the heat and let it simmer for about 15 minutes, or until the quinoa is cooked through.

3. Cool the quinoa, and then stir in the maple syrup. Divide the food into four containers, each having 1 cup fruit, ¾ cup cooked quinoa, and 1 tablespoon of sliced almonds

Nutritional information: Calories 406, Fat 16g, Protein 13g, Carbs 57g

Recipe notes

1. In case you prefer using the instant pot, you should use water instead of almond milk. Cook on high

pressure for approximately 1 minute, then allow the instant pot to release the pressure naturally.

2. If you prefer using a rice cooker, you should also use water instead of almond milk. Select the 'white rice' setting on your cooker if it has one.

3. You can store in airtight containers in the fridge for up to 4 days or in your freezer for up to 3 months

Banana Egg Pancakes

Prep time: 5 minutes

Cook time: 20 minutes

Total time: 25 minutes

Servings: 4 (4-5 pancakes each)

Ingredients

8 eggs

Nuts and fruits to serve on the side

4 bananas

Maple syrup (optional)

Directions

1. In a large bowl, mash the bananas together and then whisk in the eggs

2. In a large frying pan, heat the butter over medium heat and add in approximately ¼ cup of the pancake batter you made at a time. Cook each for about 3-4 minutes per side or until fully cooked.

3. Add the pancakes to your meal prep bowls and add the fruit. Serve with maple syrup on the side (optional)

Nutritional information: Calories 324, Fat 13g, Protein 18g, Carbs 40g

Recipe notes

4. The pancakes can be kept in the fridge for up to 5 days

5. To freeze, stack the pancakes in between wax paper and store them inside a resealable plastic bag. To reheat, microwave for 1-2 minutes.

Sweet Potato Breakfast Bowls

Prep time: 15 minutes

Cook time: 30 minutes

Total time: 45 minutes

Servings: 4

Ingredients

4 cups of sweet potatoes cut into 1/2-inch cubes

1/4 teaspoon of salt

2 diced bell peppers

4 eggs

1/4 teaspoon of salt

1 tablespoon of olive oil

2 teaspoons of chili powder

1/2 cup of water

1 cup of sliced mushrooms

1/4 cup of milk

1/2 teaspoon of chili powder

Directions

1. Toss the sweet potatoes, olive oil, salt, and chili powder in a large bowl. Add the mixture to a large pan and cook for about 10 minutes over medium heat as you stir occasionally.

2. Add ½ cup of water to the pan and then cover it. Cook for a further 10 minutes or until the sweet potatoes are fully softened. Portion the meal into 4 containers.

3. Add the mushrooms and bell peppers to the pan and add some more olive oil if necessary—Cook for approximately 5 minutes or until softened.

4. To cook the veggies, beat the eggs with salt, chili powder, and milk. Add to the pan with the vegetables

and cook for approximately 3 extra minutes or until the eggs are cooked through

5. Add to the containers that you portioned the sweet potatoes into

6. Enjoy!

Nutritional information: Calories 235, Fat 9g, Protein 10g, Carbs 32g

Recipe notes

1. You can serve by heating inside a microwave until it is steaming hot. Once hot, you can serve with avocado or salsa.

2. The sweet potatoes can be stored in the fridge for up to four days

Sheet Tray Pancakes

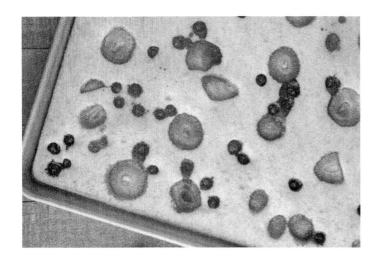

Prep time: 10 minutes

Cook time: 15 minutes

Total time: 25 minutes

Servings: 8

Ingredients

1 teaspoon of baking powder

1 ¼ cups of unsweetened applesauce

1 teaspoon of vanilla extract

Strawberry, to taste

Banana, to taste

1 ½ cups of whole wheat flour

⅔ cup of almond milk

2 eggs

Blueberry, to taste

Dark chocolate chip, to taste

Directions

1. Preheat your oven to 425F degrees. Meanwhile, mix the baking powder and whole wheat flour in a bowl.

2. Add in the vanilla extract, egg, milk, and applesauce. Mix them until well combined.

3. On a greased baking sheet, pour the pancake mix and spread it out evenly.

4. Add the topping you'd like to at this stage. either in different corners or onto the whole pan.

5. Bake it for approximately 15 minutes.

6. When done, cut into squares. Enjoy!

Nutritional information: Calories 97, Fat 2g, Protein 4g, Carbs 16g

Recipe notes

3. This recipe can be stored in a freezer for up to 1 month

High Protein Salmon Toast

Prep time: 5 minutes

Cook time: 5 minutes

Total time: 10 minutes

Servings: 1

Ingredients

2 tablespoons of whipped or labneh cream cheese

Lemon zest

2 slices of sprouted grain bread

2 oz of Trifecta salmon, shredded

Directions

1. Toast the bread and top with salmon and labneh

2. Sprinkle with the lemon zest

3. Enjoy!

Nutritional information: Calories 290, Fat 9g, Protein 23g, Carbs 28g

Protein Waffles

Prep time: 3 minutes

Cook time: 30 minutes

Total time: 33 minutes

Servings: 5

Ingredients

2/3 cup of plain Greek yogurt

1 cup of oat flour

4 large eggs

1/4 cup of milk of choice

2 scoops of plant-based protein powder (vanilla flavored)

Directions

1. Preheat your waffle maker, then whisk the eggs, milk, and yogurt in a large mixing bowl. Add the protein powder and oat flour and continue whisking until thoroughly combined.

2. Once preheated, spray the waffle iron lightly with a cooking spray, then make the waffles according to the instructions on your waffle maker. The amount of batter you should use here will also be dependent on the size of your waffle maker.

3. Cook the waffles for approximately 4-5 minutes or until crispy and golden brown.

4. Serve while still hot and top with the waffle toppings of your choice

Nutritional information: Calories 218, Fat 7g, Protein 21g, Carbs 19g

Recipe notes

1. To store keep in the freezer for up to 6 months or in the refrigerator for up to one week

Baked Omelet Muffins

Prep time: 25 minutes

Cook time: 35 minutes

Total time: 1 hour

Servings: 6

Ingredients

2 cups of finely chopped broccoli

8 large eggs

½ cup of low-fat milk

½ teaspoon of ground pepper

3 slices of chopped bacon

4 sliced scallions

1 cup of shredded Cheddar cheese

½ teaspoon of salt

Directions

1. Preheat your oven to 325 degrees F. Meanwhile, use a cooking spray to coat a 12-cup muffin tin.

2. In a large skillet, cook the bacon over medium heat for about 4-5 minutes, or until crispy. Use a slotted spoon to remove and place it on a plate lined with a paper towel. Leave the bacon fat in the pan. Add the scallions and broccoli and cook for approximately 5 minutes as you stir or until soft. Remove from the heat and let it cook for about 5 minutes. Remove from the heat and let it cool for about 5 minutes.

3. In a large bowl, whisk the eggs, pepper, salt, milk, and cheese. Stir in the broccoli mixture and bacon. Divide the mixture equally into the muffin cups you prepared earlier.

4. Bake until they are firm to touch, for about 25-30 minutes. Let it sit for about 5 minutes before you remove the muffins from the tin.

Nutritional information (2 mini omelets): Calories 212, Fat 14.5g, Protein 15.7g, Carbs 4.6g

Recipe notes

1. For meal prep, wrap the omelets in plastic wrap and store them in a freezer for up to 1 month or in the refrigerator for up to 3 days.

2. To reheat the muffins, thaw if need be, then remove the plastic wrap. Wrap them in a paper towel and microwave on a high setting for about 20-30 seconds.

Protein Pancakes

Prep time: 5 minutes

Cook time:10 minutes

Total time:15 minutes

Servings:15

Ingredients

1/3 cup of plain Greek yogurt (2% fat or higher)

1/2 cup and 1 tablespoon of oat flour

3 large eggs

2 tablespoons of maple syrup

1 scoop of 30g whey protein powder (vanilla or unflavored)

Directions

1. Whisk the eggs in a large mixing bowl, then add the maple syrup and yogurt. Whisk until well combined, then add the protein powder and oat flour. Stir until well combined.

2. Over medium heat, preheat a skillet. Use cooking spray to coat and pour the batter depending on the size you desire (2-3 tablespoons for a medium-sized pancake).

3. Cook for less than a minute on one side, then flip over when bubbles start appearing, but the batter is still wet. Do not wait for brown edges. Cook for a few extra seconds (around 10 seconds), and the pancakes are ready (cooking for longer dries out the whey).

Nutritional information: Calories 47, Fat 1g, Protein 4g, Carbs 5g

Recipe notes

1. Store in airtight containers in a freezer for up to 3 months or the fridge for up to 3 days.

2. You can use agave or honey in place of maple syrup.

3. If your first pancakes come out dry, try adding more a little more water or milk. You can also add a little more pumpkin puree, apple sauce, mashed banana, or Greek yogurt.

Egg Muffins with Cauliflower Rice, Ham, and Kale

Prep time: 10 minutes

Cook time: 20 minutes

Total time: 30 minutes

Servings: 6

Ingredients

3 large eggs

3/4 cup of heavily packed pasture-raised ham, cut into bite-sized cubes

1 cup of cauliflower (cut into bite-sized pieces)

1 cup of lightly packed spinach or kale, torn into bite-sized pieces

Salt & pepper to taste

Directions

1. Preheat your oven to 400 degrees. Meanwhile, use cooking spray generously to coat a muffin tin, then set it aside.

2. Process the cauliflower in a small food processor until it is fully broken down and looks like rice. Set it aside.

3. Whisk the eggs in a large bowl and then add in the cauliflower rice, ham, kale, and season with a pinch of pepper and salt. Mix well.

4. Divide the mixture you made into 6 muffin tins and then bake until the eggs are well set or for approximately 20 minutes.

5. Once done, let it cool, then enjoy!

Nutritional information: Calories 76, Fat 4.3g, Protein 6.9g, Carbs 2.8g

Bacon-Wrapped Egg Cups

Prep time: 8 minutes

Cook time: 22 minutes

Total time: 30 minutes

Servings: 12

Ingredients

12 large eggs

12 strips of bacon

pepper, to taste

Directions

1. Preheat your oven to 400 degrees F. Meanwhile, use the coconut oil to spray a non-stick muffin tin, then set it aside

2. Create a kind of basket using one piece of bacon per muffin. Place the bacon on the insides of each muffin in such a way that it covers the sides completely. Use a pair of kitchen scissors to cut the excess bacon. Use the excess piece as the bottom of the 'bacon basket.'

3. Once you've created all the bacon wraps, place them in the oven and bake at 400 degrees F for approximately 7 minutes. Remove them from the oven before they start to get crispy.

4. Crack an egg inside each of the bacon baskets. Bake for a further 10-15 minutes (depends on how runny you'd like your eggs to be).

5. Season with pepper and serve

Nutritional information: Calories 115, Fat 8g, Protein 9g, Carbs 0g

Egg and Sausage McMuffin

Prep time: 20 minutes

Cook time: 20 minutes

Total time: 40 minutes

Servings: 6

Ingredients

1 tablespoon of olive oil, divided

1 tablespoon of fennel seeds

1 teaspoon of garlic powder

1/2 teaspoon of pepper

6 slices of cheddar cheese

1 lb. of ground turkey or chicken

1 teaspoon of paprika

1 teaspoon of salt

6 eggs

6 English muffins

Directions

1. Mix together the garlic powder, ground turkey, paprika, pepper, and salt in a large bowl. Create 6 patties from this.

2. Over medium-high heat, preheat 1 tablespoon of olive oil, then add the patties to the skillet. Cook for about 5 minutes per side or until the patties are fully cooked through.

3. Meanwhile, use a toaster to toast the English muffins lightly, then add the cheese slices to the bottom of the muffins. Remove the sausages you made from the heat, and then add them on top of the cheese slices that are now set on the English muffins.

4. Wipe the frying pan using a paper towel and then spray it using a cooking spray of your choice. Heat it on medium-low. Crack the eggs onto egg rings. Ensure that the rings touch the bottom of the skillet firmly so that your eggs can have a well-rounded shape, then break the yolk.

5. Cover the skillet with a lid and let the eggs cook until they are firm, for approximately 4-5 minutes. Add the eggs on top of the sausage and top with the English muffin bun.

6. Enjoy!

Nutritional information: Calories 406, Fat 19g, Protein 31g, Carbs 26g

Peanut Butter Protein Pancakes

Prep time: 5 minutes

Cook time: 20 minutes

Total time: 25 minutes

Servings: 6

Ingredients

1 large egg

1/4 cup of peanut butter

1 large over-ripen banana

1/2 cup of milk of choice

1/4 cup of rolled or quick oats

2 scoops of plant-based protein powder

2 teaspoons of baking powder

Avocado or coconut oil for frying

Directions

1. Add all the ingredients into a food processor or blender and process until smooth

2. On low medium heat, preheat a large cast-iron skillet. Swirl oil to coat. Divide the batter into 3 large pancakes and cook each for around 3-5 minutes per side (or until the batter on top isn't so jiggly), and then flip over to the other side. Cook for another 3-5 minutes. Repeat with other batches.

3. Serve hot with your desired toppings

Nutritional information: Calories 147, Fat 7g, Protein 13g, Carbs 10g

Recipe notes

1. Store the pancakes in an airtight container in your freezer for up to 3 months or refrigerate for up to 5 days.

Overnight Oats

Prep time: 5 minutes

Cook time: 2 hours

Total time: 2 hours 5 minutes

Servings: 1

Ingredients

Base Recipe

1/2 cup of milk (oat milk, coconut, almond milk, soya milk, skimmed milk, or semi-skimmed milk)

1 tablespoon of a sweetener of your choice (optional)

1/2 cup of rolled oats

1/2 tablespoon of chia seeds

Berries version

1/2 cup of mixed berries (strawberries, blueberries, raspberries)

1 teaspoon of honey (maple syrup for a vegan version)

Walnut and coffee version

1 tablespoon of maple syrup

2 tablespoons of Greek yogurt (coconut yogurt for a vegan version)

1 teaspoon of instant coffee

5 half walnuts

Double Chocolate version

2/3 tablespoon of cocoa powder

2 tablespoons of coconut yogurt

5-8 roasted hazelnuts

1 tablespoon of maple syrup

1 teaspoon of Nutella

A few chocolate chips or raw cacao nibs

Apple Pie version

1 teaspoon of cinnamon

1 small apple

1 tablespoon of maple syrup

5 pecans

Peanut Butter version

2 tablespoons of peanut butter (salted or natural, crunchy or creamy)

A handful of peanuts or any other nuts

Fresh fruits (raspberries, bananas, blueberries), optional

A few chocolate chips or raw cacao nibs

Tropical version

2 tablespoons of coconut yogurt

Mango (freshly sliced)

Coconut flakes

1 tablespoon of maple syrup

Fresh slices of banana

Directions

Base recipe

1. In an 8oz container or glass jar, place the chia seeds and rolled oats and stir using a spoon.

2. Add the milk and a sweetener of your choice and mix thoroughly.

3. Cover the container using a wrap or lid and store in the fridge for a minimum of 2 hours (overnight is better as it gives a better texture).

4. On the following day, open the container and add the desired toppings.

Berry version

1. For the berry version of this recipe, ensure that you add honey in the base recipe above the previous night.

2. On the next day, add the berries on top. If you want to eat it, add oats and warm, then ensure that you warm up the oats first before adding the berries.

Walnut and coffee version

1. Add the rolled oats, chia seeds, and instant coffee, and give them a good mix. Add the milk and maple syrup. You can also add a shot of espresso in place of the instant coffee with a little less milk.

2. On the next day, top with walnuts and Greek yogurt

Apple pie version

1. Add the chia seeds, rolled oats, and cinnamon and mix them thoroughly. Add the milk and maple syrup.

2. If you plan to eat it warm and would like to have more of an apple pie taste, then you should add the apples on your oats immediately you take them out of the fridge.

3. Warm the apples and oats in the microwave for approximately 45-60 seconds (the point is not to heat but rather to warm).

Double chocolate version

1. Add the chia seeds, rolled oats, and cocoa powder and mix them well. Add the milk and maple syrup.

2. On the following day, top with cacao nibs, crunchy toasted hazelnuts, coconut yogurt, and some Nutella.

Peanut butter version

1. Mix the base recipe as shown, then on the next day, top with raw cacao nibs, peanut butter, and nuts. You can also add some fresh fruits.

Tropical version

1. Mix the base recipe. However, for a more 'pina colada' taste, ensure that you use coconut milk. If you are not going to warm it up later, then you can add 1 tablespoon of coconut yogurt to your base recipe before putting it in the refrigerator. This brings a creamier texture.

2. On the following day, top with banana slices, coconut flakes, mango slices, and the remaining coconut flakes.

Nutritional information: Calories 240, Fat 7g, Protein 8g, Carbs 37.5g

Recipe notes

1. To warm up your overnight oats, you should microwave them in your microwave for around 4-60 seconds or simply transfer them to a saucepan and heat. If the oats start thickening, then add some more liquid.

2. Store the overnight oats in the fridge for up to 5 days

3. The nutritional information is based on the base recipe without toppings or sweeteners.

Tex Mex Breakfast Quesadillas

Prep time: 20 minutes

Cook time: 30 minutes

Total time: 50 minutes

Servings: 16

Ingredients

1 package of breakfast sausages

8 flour tortillas

1/2 each of green, red and yellow bell pepper, diced finely

Tomato, cilantro & lime wedges for garnish

1 tablespoon of olive oil

3 scrambled eggs

2 cups of tex mex cheese, pre-shredded

Pepper and salt to taste

1 small red onion, diced finely

Directions

1. In a large pan, heat the olive oil over medium-high heat. Cook the sausage according to the instructions on the package. Once fully cooked, transfer to a plate lined with a paper towel. Once cooled, slice up.

2. Meanwhile, in a small bowl, mix the eggs together. Add them to a pan and cook for 2-3 minutes, or until scrambled. Remove it from the heat and transfer to a small bowl.

3. Meanwhile, dice up the onion and peppers until fine. Top each of the half tortillas with the sliced sausages, a bit of cheese, veggies, and a bit of egg. Top with some more cheese and fold over. Over medium-low heat, cook the quesadillas in a large frying pan, two at a

time. Cook each side for around 5-7 minutes or until the cheese melts.

4. Cut each of the quesadillas half wise and serve. Enjoy!

Nutritional information: Calories 211, Fat 15g, Protein 10g, Carbs 9g

Recipe notes

1. To store, place between wax paper and keep inside a large resealable plastic bag and freeze. When you are ready to eat, remove one at a time each and microwave them for a few minutes, then serve. You can also reheat inside an oven if you want a crispier tortilla.

Salmon Eggs Benedict with Avocado Hollandaise

Prep time: 5 minutes

Cook time: 5 minutes

Total time: 10 minutes

Servings: 1

Ingredients

1 english muffin

½ ripe avocado

2 teaspoons of lemon juice

1 egg

4oz of trifecta salmon

1 fresh spinach

1 ½ tablespoon of extra virgin olive oil

1/3 cup of water

Salt and pepper to taste

Directions

1. To prepare the hollandaise, combine 1/3 cup of water, 2 teaspoons of lemon juice, 2 pinches of pepper and salt, and ½ a ripe avocado in a blender. Process them until smooth (about 1 ½ minute). As you continue blending, add 1 tablespoon of olive oil and blend until well combined. Set them aside.

2. Add a handful of spinach, ½ a tablespoon of olive oil, pepper, and salt to a small saucepan. Flip the spinach until it is well coated with olive oil and cook until the spinach becomes wilted. Set aside.

3. Heat the trifecta salmon in a small non-stick pan and heat over low heat. When the salmon is warm enough

on touch, increase the heat to medium. Wait until the salmon filet crisps and browns lightly.

4. As the salmon continues heating, toast the eggs and English muffin

5. Place a part of wilted spinach on the English muffin. Layer the browned salmon and the poached egg. Top with red pepper flakes and avocado hollandaise.

Nutritional information: Calories 450, Fat 22g, Protein 33g, Carbs 27g

Vegan Freezer Breakfast Burritos

Cook time: 30 minutes

Total time: 30 minutes

Servings: 6

Ingredients

1 package (14-ounce) of extra-firm water-packed tofu, crumbled and drained

1 teaspoon of ground cumin

1 can (15-ounce) of rinsed, reduced-sodium black beans

4 sliced scallions

¼ cup of chopped fresh cilantro

2 tablespoons of divided avocado oil

2 teaspoons of chili powder

¼ teaspoon of salt

1 cup of thawed frozen corn

½ cup of prepared fresh salsa

6 (8-inch) of tortillas or whole-wheat wraps

Directions

1. In a large skillet, heat 1 tablespoon of oil over medium heat. Add the salt, cumin, chili powder, tofu, and cook as you stir. Continue until the tofu is browned nicely (around 10-12 minutes). Transfer to a bowl.

2. Add the remaining tablespoon of oil to the pan. Add the scallions, beans, and corn, and cook as you stir until the scallions soften (around 3 minutes). Return the tofu to the pan. Add the cilantro, salsa and cook as you stir continuously for around 2 minutes, or until heated through.

3. If you are going to serve immediately, warm the wraps/tortillas. If you are going to store them in a freezer, then don't warm them. Divide the bean mixture equally among the tortillas, ensuring that you

spread them in an even layer over the bottom third of your tortillas. Roll them snugly and tuck the ends.

4. Serve immediately. Enjoy!

Nutritional information: Calories 329, Fat 10.4g, Protein 15.2g, Carbs 44.8g

Recipe notes

1. To store, wrap each burrito using foil and keep them in the freezer for up to 3 months.

2. To reheat using a microwave, remove the foil and cover using a paper towel. Microwave on high setting until hot (approximately 1 ½ to 2 minutes).

Protein-Packed Breakfast Burritos

Prep time: 5 minutes

Cook time: 10 minutes

Total time: 15 minutes

Servings: 4

Ingredients

A splash of milk

1 tablespoon of minced garlic

1/2 medium, finely minced red onion

Pepper and salt, to taste

8 large eggs

1 tablespoon of olive oil

1 medium finely minced red pepper

4 pieces of thick-cut bacon, cooked until crispy

4 Flat-out Flatbreads

Directions

1. In a medium sauce-pan, place the minced garlic and olive oil. Cook on medium-high heat until the oil is heated. Meanwhile, whisk a splash of milk and 8 eggs in a large bowl. Set aside.

2. Add the onion and red pepper to the pan and sauté until the onions start turning translucent. Add in the eggs and sauté for an additional 3-5 minutes, or until cooked.

3. Place a piece of cooked bacon and ¼ of the egg mixture on a flat-out flatbread. Sprinkle with some cheese, and then wrap it snugly. Enjoy!

Nutritional information: Calories 352, Fat 20g, Protein 25g, Carbs 22g

Vegetarian Black Bean Breakfast Burritos

Prep time: 15 minutes

Cook time: 25 minutes

Total time: 40 minutes

Servings: 8

Ingredients

For the Sweet Potatoes

2 tablespoons of olive oil

1 teaspoon of chili powder

Sea salt, to taste

3 cups sweet of chunked and peeled potatoes

1 teaspoon of garlic powder

1 teaspoon of ground cumin

For the Black Bean Mash

2 tablespoons of tahini (or 2 tablespoons of olive oil)

2 tablespoons of lime juice

1/4 cup of olive oil

2 ½ cups of black beans

1 teaspoon of cumin

1/4 teaspoon of sea salt

For the Eggs

A splash of milk of choice

1/2 finely diced yellow onion

8 large eggs

1/2 tablespoon of EVOO

Salt and pepper, to taste

Other

8 tablespoons of green chiles

8 tablespoons of corn

8 whole-wheat tortillas

8 tablespoons of harissa sauce (or salsa)

8 tablespoons of chopped onion

Directions

Sweet potatoes

1. Preheat your oven to 400 degrees F. On a baking pan, drizzle around 2 tablespoons of olive oil.

2. Dice the sweet potatoes into 1-inch chunks to prep them. Spread them on the pan and season them with spices as desired.

3. Toss the sweet potatoes using your hands to cover them with spices and olive oil. Place in the oven and roast until you can pierce easily using a fork (approximately 20-25 minutes). Set aside.

Black bean mash

1. Use a high-speed food processor to process all the ingredients for the black bean mash on a high setting until smooth. If need be, add some more olive oil to thin out the paste. Set aside.

Eggs

1. In a large saucepan, heat about ½ a tablespoon of EVOO. Add in the yellow onion and sauté until it begins to turn translucent.

2. In a large bowl, crack 8 eggs and then add a splash of milk. Whisk thoroughly. Add into the pan and cook. Scrape the sides occasionally using a spatula until cooked to your liking—season with pepper and salt to taste.

Assembling your burritos

1. Lay the 8 tortillas and spread a tablespoon of harissa sauce and a tablespoon of black mean mash onto each.

2. Add the egg, sweet potatoes, tablespoon of green chiles, tablespoon of corn, and a tablespoon of chopped onion.

3. Wrap it just like a burrito and eat it immediately.

Nutritional information: Calories 441, Fat 15g, Protein 16g, Carbs 60g

Recipe notes

1. To store, wrap your burritos in tin foil, then wrap them inside a plastic wrap and squeeze out as much air as you can to prevent freezer burn. Keep in the freezer for up to 3 months.

Egg and Avocado Breakfast

Prep time: 20 minutes

Cook time: 35 minutes

Total time: 55 minutes

Servings: 4

Ingredients

6 large eggs

2 cloves of garlic, minced

4 cups of chopped kale

1 halved avocado, sliced, peeled, and seeded

1/2 cup of brown rice

2 tablespoons of olive oil

1/4 teaspoon of crushed red pepper flakes (optional)

1/4 cup of freshly grated Parmesan

Directions

1. Cook rice in a large saucepan with 1 cup of water (according to the instructions on the package). Set aside.

2. Cover the eggs with water in a large saucepan by 1 inch. Bring it to boil and cook for around 1 minute. Remove the eggs from the heat and cover with a lid that fits tightly. Set them aside for around 8-10 minutes. Drain the water well and let the eggs cool before you peel them and halve them.

3. In a large skillet, heat the olive oil over medium-high heat. Add red pepper flakes and garlic (if you are going to use them). Cook as you constantly stir until it becomes fragrant (approximately 1-2 minutes). Stir in the kale until it becomes wilted (around 5-6 minutes). Stir in the parmesan.

4. Place the kale, eggs, avocado, and rice into meal prep containers

Nutritional information: Calories 392, Fat 24.9g, Protein 14.3g, Carbs 30.6g

Simple Toast With Avocado And Poached Egg

Prep time: 5 minutes

Cook time: 5 minutes

Total time: 10 minutes

Servings: 1

Ingredients

2 slices of whole-grain bread

2 tablespoons of shaved parmesan cheese

Fresh herbs (thyme, parsley, or basil) for topping

2 eggs

1/3 avocado

Salt and pepper for topping

Quartered heirloom tomatoes for serving

Directions

1. Set a pot of water on heat and bring it to boil (enough water to cover eggs when laying in the bottom). Meanwhile, take two mason jar lids and drop the outer metal rims into the pot, such that they are lying flat at the bottom. When the water boils, turn off the heat and crack your eggs carefully and directly into each of the rims. Cover the pot and poach for approximately 5 minutes for a semi-soft yolk, 4:30 for soft, and 4 for super soft yolks.

2. As the eggs are cooking, toast your bread. When done, smash the avocado on each toast piece. When the eggs are ready, lift the eggs out of the water using a spatula. Pull the rim off the eggs gently and set the poached eggs on top of the toast. Sprinkle with salt, parmesan cheese, fresh herbs, and pepper.

3. Serve with the quartered heirloom tomatoes.

Nutritional information: Calories 393, Fat 20.4 g, Protein 23.3g, Carbs 30.1g

Recipe notes

4. To help the eggs stay together in the water, you can try adding a teaspoon of vinegar to the water before it boils.

5. To reduce the fat content in this recipe, just use egg white instead of whole eggs and reduce the avocado you use.

Main Meal Recipes

Simple Turkey Chili

Prep time: 15 minutes

Cook time: 45 minutes

Total time: 60 minutes

Servings: 8

Ingredients

1 ½ teaspoon of olive oil

1 chopped onion

1 can (28 ounces) of crushed tomatoes

1 tablespoon of minced garlic

½ teaspoon of paprika

½ teaspoon of salt

1 pound of ground turkey

2 cups of water

1 can (16 ounces) of drained, rinsed, and crushed kidney beans

2 tablespoons of chili powder

½ teaspoon of ground cayenne pepper

½ teaspoon of dried oregano

½ teaspoon of ground cumin

½ teaspoon of ground black pepper

Directions

1. In a large pot, heat the oil over medium heat. Place the turkey in the pot and allow it to cook until it browns evenly. Stir in the onion and continue cooking until tender

2. Pour the water into the pot and mix in the garlic, tomatoes, and kidney beans. Season with cumin, salt, pepper, cayenne pepper, paprika, chili powder, and oregano. Bring it to a boil. Reduce the heat to low, cover, and allow it to simmer for 30 minutes.

3. Serve and enjoy!

Nutritional information: Calories 185, Fat 6.1g, Protein 16.4g, Carbs 18.8g

Chicken Taco Soup

Prep time: 5 minutes

Cook time: 7 minutes

Total time: 12 minutes

Servings: 8

Ingredients

1 chopped onion

Bottle of beer (12 oz) (can be substituted with broth)

15 oz can of rinsed pinto or chili beans

15 oz can of rinsed black beans

15 oz can of drained corn

8 oz can of tomato sauce

28 oz cans of diced tomatoes undrained

1 oz packet of taco seasoning

3 boneless, skinless chicken breasts

Optional Toppings

Sour cream and shredded cheese

Directions

1. Prepare your slow cooker and place the tomatoes, tomato sauce, corn, beans, chopped onions, and bear into it. Mix thoroughly.

2. Add the taco seasoning and stir well to mix.

3. Add the chicken breasts into the mixture, ensuring that you press down until they are fully covered by the mixture.

4. Cook on low for approximately 7 hours.

5. Once ready, remove the chicken from the pot and use 2 forks to shred it.

6. Stir it back into your crockpot.

7. Serve the soup with the optional toppings or as it is.

Nutritional information: Calories 234, Fat 3g, Protein 17g, Carbs 34g

Recipe notes

1. To make this recipe vegetarian-friendly, omit the chicken and add 2 cans of chickpeas, white beans, or kidney beans.

2. Despite using beer, this final result does not have a beer taste.

3. Use beer instead of soup to make this recipe a zero-point weight watcher.

Kung Pao Chicken

Prep time: 10 minutes

Cook time: 15 minutes

Total time: 20 minutes

Servings: 4

Ingredients

1/4 cup of tamari (coconut aminos or soy sauce)

1 tablespoon of sriracha

2 tablespoons of honey

1 tablespoon of minced garlic

1 teaspoon of sesame oil

1 tablespoon of chili garlic paste

1 lb. of skinless, boneless chicken breast

1/8 teaspoon of ground pepper

1 lb. of fresh green beans, with ends trimmed

2 tablespoons of olive oil

Pinch of salt

2 teaspoons of cornstarch

Optional toppings

Peanuts

Sesame seeds

Directions

1. Start by preparing the Kung Pao sauce. Mix the soy sauce, minced garlic, sriracha, sesame oil, honey, and chili garlic paste. Set aside.

2. Prep your chicken by slicing it thinly into small bite-sized pieces.

3. In a large pan, heat 1 tablespoon of olive oil over medium-high heat. Add the diced chicken and season it with pepper and salt. Sauté for approximately 3-4 minutes to cook it partially. Remove it from the heat and set it aside.

4. Add another tablespoon of olive oil into the pan and add the green beans. Sauté them for approximately 3-4 minutes over medium-high heat. Once the green beans are cooked partially, add the chicken back to the pan and mix well.

5. Place the lid back onto the skillet and let the food steam for 2-3 minutes. This allows the green beans to cook and also ensures that you cook the chicken fully.

6. Remove the lid and mix again. Scoot the green beans and chicken to one side of your pan and add the sauce to that space. Sprinkle about 2 teaspoons of cornstarch over the sauce and whisk them over medium-high heat

7. Mix everything together

8. Serve with peanuts and sesame seeds over your favorite grain

Nutritional information: Calories 282, Fat 11 g, Protein 34g, Carbs 20g

Recipe notes

1. If you would like this recipe to have a hotter and spicier taste, double the chili paste or sriracha

Avocado Chicken Salad

Prep time: 5 minutes

Cook time: 0 minutes

Total time: 5 minutes

Servings:

Ingredients

For the chicken salad:

2 tablespoons of plain yogurt

3/4 cup of precooked, shredded chicken

1/4 avocado

1 teaspoon of lemon juice

For the sandwich:

Sunflower sprouts or a handful of lettuce

1 whole-wheat English muffin

2 slices of tomato

Directions

1. Mash the avocado with lemon juice and yogurt in a small bowl until fully combined

2. Add the chicken into the bowl and use a spoon to mix until the chicken is fully coated.

3. Prepare a bed of lettuce and serve the chicken on top of it, or split it up on top of two English muffins with sunflower sprouts and a slice of tomato. Enjoy!

Nutritional information: Calories 425, Fat 14.9g, Protein 39.6g, Carbs 34.6g

Light Mongolian Beef

Prep time: 10 minutes

Cook time: 10 minutes

Total time: 20 minutes

Servings: 4

Ingredients

1 pound of thinly sliced steak (flank or sirloin)

1 tablespoon of hoisin sauce

1 teaspoon of chili sauce like sambal oelek

1 teaspoon grated ginger

1/3 beef broth or water

1/4 cup of sliced green onion

1 tablespoon of oil

3 tablespoons of soy sauce

1 tablespoon of brown sugar

1 clove of grated garlic

1 tablespoon of cornstarch

1 teaspoon of sesame oil

Directions

1. In a pan, heat the oil over medium-high heat and add the beef. Sauté for around 2-4 minutes or until just cooked.

2. Mix the hoisin sauce, soy sauce, chili sauce, brown sugar, chili sauce, and ginger, and add the mixture to the pan. Mix the water and cornstarch and also add them to the pan—Cook for approximately 1 minute, or until it starts to thicken.

3. Remove from the heat and add the sesame oil. Mix well and then serve over noodles or white rice, quinoa or noodles and garnish with green onions.

Nutritional information: Calories 354, Fat 23g, Protein 22g, Carbs 9g

Recipe notes

1. You can also add some veggies such as peppers, peas, and broccoli to the mix

Greek Marinated Chicken

Prep time: 45 minutes

Cook time: 60 minutes

Total time: 1hour 45 minutes

Servings:

Ingredients

1 cup of plain yogurt

4 cloves of minced garlic

1 medium lemon

freshly cracked pepper

3 1/2 to 4 lbs. of chicken pieces

2 tablespoon of olive oil

1/2 tablespoon of dried oregano

1/2 teaspoon of salt

1/4 bunch of fresh parsley

Directions

1. To make the marinade, combine minced garlic, olive oil, yogurt, oregano, freshly cracked pepper, and salt into a bowl. Scrape a thin layer of the yellow zest using a zester or a fine holed cheese grater from the lemon skin and put it in the bowl. Squeeze half of the lemon and add the juice to the bowl. Stir well until all the ingredients are combined. Chop a big handful of parsley (about ¼ of a bunch) and stir it into the marinade.

2. To a gallon-sized lock bag, add the marinade and the chicken pieces. Ensure that you remove as much air as possible from the bag. Close it tightly and massage it to mix the contents, ensuring that the chicken is

coated well. Refrigerate it for around 30 minutes. When done, you can either preheat your oven to 375 degrees and bake the chicken or cook it on a grill.

3. To bake the chicken, place the pieces on a 9x13 casserole dish. Bake it in the oven until it turns golden brown on top (around 45-60 minutes).

Nutritional information: Calories 566.3, Fat 38.6g, Protein 52.3g, Carbs 3.5g

Recipe notes

1. This recipe has an extra garlicky flavor. If you do not like a strong garlic taste, you should consider using 2 cloves of garlic.

Jerk Chicken Bowls

Prep time: 20 minutes

Cook time: 10 minutes

Total time: 30 minutes

Servings: 4

Ingredients

1.5 pounds of chicken breast (cut into 1-inch pieces)

2 cups of diced pineapple

1/4 cup of chopped cilantro

1 5 oz package of cooked yellow rice

1 tablespoon of Jamaican Jerk Seasoning

1/2 cup of diced red onion

1 can of drained and rinsed black beans

Directions

1. Mix the red onion, cilantro, and pineapple together in a small bowl. Set aside.

2. Sprinkle the jerk seasoning over your chicken and stir well to coat.

3. Using a non-stick cooking spray, coat your pan and add the chicken. Cook it for about 6-7 minutes over medium heat until it cooks through.

4. Spoon the black beans, pineapple salsa, rice, and black beans into 4 containers or simply serve in a bowl. enjoy

Nutritional information: Calories 319, Fat 4g, Protein 42g, Carbs 26g

Creamy Spinach Chicken with Zucchini Noodles

Prep time: 10 minutes

Cook time: 20 minutes

Total time: 30 minutes

Servings: 3

Ingredients

2 teaspoons of olive oil

5 cloves of finely diced garlic

1/3 cup (80ml) of chicken broth

1 3/4 cups of heavy cream

3 cups of baby spinach leaves

1 tablespoon of fresh, chopped parsley

3 small chicken breasts, horizontally sliced to make cutlets (or 2 large chicken breasts)

2 tablespoons of butter

1 small diced yellow onion

5 ounces (150g) of jarred sun-dried tomato in oil, drained

Pepper and salt, to taste

1/2 cup of grated Parmesan

3 cups of zucchini noodles

Directions

1. Start by steaming the zucchini noodles in a large bowl in the microwave for 3-4 minutes, covered, with ½ cup of water. Once done, drain it and set it aside. You

can skip this step if you like your zucchini noodles raw or if you would like to cook them in the creamy sauce.

2. In a large skillet, heat oil over medium heat. Season the large chicken with pepper and salt on both sides and sear in the hot pan until cooked through - approximately 5 minutes on each side. Once done, remove from the pan and set aside.

3. In the same pan, melt the butter in the remaining juices. Add the garlic and fry for about 1 minute (until fragrant). Add the onion and stir fry it until it turns translucent. Add the sun-dried tomatoes, then proceed to fry for around 1-2 minutes to allow them to release their flavor. Pour in the chicken broth and let the sauce slowly reduce down.

4. Turn the heat to low and then add the heavy cream. Bring it to a gentle simmer as you stir occasionally—season with pepper and salt.

5. Add the baby spinach then let it to wilt in the sauce. Add the parmesan cheese. Give the cream sauce an extra minute to simmer. You want to makes sure that the cheese has melted all through.

6. Add the chicken breasts back into the pan and sprinkle with parsley. Spoon the sauce over the

chicken. If you skipped step 1 and you'd like to cook the zucchini noodles in the sauce, then scoot the chicken to one side and toss in the spiralized zucchini noodles. Cook for 2 minutes as you stir regularly. Serve or divide zucchini noodles into meal prep containers and top with the chicken. When you are ready to eat, just reheat in a microwave.

Nutritional information: Calories 740.35, Fat 52.23 g, Protein 52.61g, Carbs 17.07g

Chickpea Quinoa Salad

Prep time: 15 minutes

Cook time: 10 minutes

Total time: 25 minutes

Servings: 2

Ingredients

1 cup of cooked quinoa

1/2 cup of pomegranate arils

1/2 cup of chopped red onion

1 can (15 ounces) of well rinsed and drained chickpeas

1 cup of chopped English cucumber

1/4 cup of finely chopped parsley

2 hardboiled eggs

The salad dressing

Juice of 1 lemon

2 teaspoons of dried oregano

3 tablespoons of olive oil

1 tablespoon of red wine vinegar

Directions

1. Start by tossing the cooked quinoa, pomegranate seeds, chickpeas, red onion, and cucumber together in a large bowl to make the chickpea quinoa salad.

2. Prepare the dressing by adding the chickpeas dressing ingredients into a mason jar and shake thoroughly until well combined.

3. Divide your salad equally into 2 meal prep containers. Add a lemon wedge, halved boiled eggs, and season with pepper and salt to your liking.

4. When you are ready to eat, just add the dressing to your chickpea quinoa salad and stir together.

Nutritional information: Calories 638.69, Fat 39.27g, Protein 16.6g, Carbs 57.51g

General Tso's Chickpeas

Prep time: 10 minutes

Cook time: 10 minutes

Total time: 20 minutes

Servings: 3

Ingredients

For marinating the chickpeas:

1 tablespoon of dry sherry or mirin

1 tablespoon of soy sauce (or tamari for GF)

1 ½ cups of cooked chickpeas, rinsed and drained

For the General Tso's sauce:

1 ½ tablespoon of tomato paste

1 tablespoon of low-sodium soy sauce (or tamari for GF)

4 teaspoon of coconut sugar (or any other sugar)

1 teaspoon of toasted sesame oil

1 teaspoon of cornstarch

6 tablespoons of low-sodium vegetable broth

1/2 tablespoon of natural peanut butter

1 tablespoon of rice vinegar

2 teaspoons of sriracha or any other chili sauce

1 teaspoon of prepared mustard (use nuttier or grainier mustards)

1/8 teaspoon of freshly ground white pepper or black pepper

For the Tso's chickpeas stir-fry:

1 thinly sliced shallot (or 1/4 of a large onion)

1 red bell pepper, cut into thin strips

2 cloves of minced garlic

Marinated chickpeas

Cooked rice, for serving (optional)

1 tablespoon of neutral oil

1 large broccoli crown, cut into florets

1 teaspoon of minced ginger

General Tso's sauce

Green onions, fresh red onion, and sesame seeds, for serving(optional)

Directions

To marinate the chickpeas

1. In a bowl, stir together the mirin and soy sauce, then add the chickpeas. Let them sit for around 10 minutes. Meanwhile, prepare the sauce and vegetables.

The sauce

2. Whisk all the sauce ingredients together and set aside

Stir-fry

3. If you would like to garnish your dish with extra diced red onion, then put the amount you'd like to use to garnish in a small bowl with water now. This allows it to mellow out its flavor

4. In a large skillet, heat oil over high heat. When hot, add the onion and stir continuously. Add the garlic, broccoli, ginger, and bell pepper strips.

5. Stir in General Tso's sauce. Drain your chickpeas and stir them in. Cook for an extra 1-2 minutes as you continue to stir frequently or until the sauce has coated the veggies and chickpeas and is hot throughout. Add more chili sauce and soy sauce to taste.

6. If desired, serve over rice and garnish with sesame seeds, green onions, chickpeas, and the soaked red onion (drain it first)

Nutritional information: Calories 253, Fat 10g, Protein 8g, Carbs 35g

Recipe notes

1. For this recipe, you'll need to prep all your ingredients before cooking since you'll need to stir all through.

2. You can substitute sherry or mirin with rice vinegar.

3. If you prefer to use bright yellow mustard, then reduce the amount of mustard to ½ teaspoon.

Chicken And Avocado Burritos

Prep time: 15 minutes

Cook time: 5 minutes

Total time: 20 minutes

Servings: 4

Ingredients

1 pound of cooked chicken, shredded or sliced

1 cup of shredded Monterey Jack cheese

1/4 cup of Greek yogurt or sour cream

4 warmed burrito sized tortillas (for gluten-free, use corn tortillas)

1 large diced avocado

1/4 cup of salsa Verde

2 tablespoons of chopped cilantro

Directions

1. Assemble your burritos. Optionally, you can toast and enjoy!

Nutritional information: Calories 519, Fat 24g, Protein 40g, Carbs 37.2g

Recipe notes

1. You can also use tequila lime grilled chicken, taco lime grilled chicken, or cilantro lime grilled chicken in place of the plain chicken

Spicy Chicken and Sweet Potato

Prep time: 15 minutes

Cook time: 30 minutes

Total time: 45 minutes

Servings: 8

Ingredients

3 tablespoons of spicy seasoning mix

3 peeled and diced sweet potatoes

Freshly cracked pepper and coarse sea salt

2 lbs. of skinless, boneless chicken breasts, cut into small pieces

A few tablespoons of olive oil

5–6 cups of broccoli florets (broccolini ftw)

Hummus or avocado or lemon juice or olive oil or chives for serving

Directions

1. Preheat your oven to 435 degrees F. Meanwhile, toss the chicken pieces with a quick stream of olive oil and the spices, then stir well to combine. Keep it in the fridge for around 30 minutes as you prep other ingredients.

2. On a sheet pan, arrange the veggies and drizzle with some olive oil, and sprinkle with some salt. On a separate sheet pan, arrange the chicken.

3. Bake all the ingredients for approximately 12-15 minutes. Remove the chicken and broccoli, and then

stir in the sweet potatoes. Continue roasting the remaining ingredients for an extra 15 minutes

4. Once done, divide your servings into containers for meal prep.

Nutritional information: Calories 237, Fat 6.7g, Protein 28g, Carbs 15.3g

Healthy Cashew Chicken Casserole

Prep time: 15 minutes

Cook time: 55 minutes

Total time: 1 hour 10 minutes

Servings: 4 - 6

Ingredients

1 cup of minced yellow onion

1 lb. of skinless, boneless chicken breast, diced into bite-sized pieces

1 tablespoon of minced garlic

1/2 tablespoon of minced fresh ginger or ginger paste

1 cup of cashews (roasted or raw)

1 cup of rinsed and uncooked white quinoa

2 medium-sized bell peppers, chopped into bite-sized pieces (any color)

1/2 cup of hoisin sauce

2 tablespoons of low sodium tamari or soy sauce

1.25 cups of water

Optional garnishes sesame seeds and/or green onion

Directions

1. Start by preheating your oven to 375 degrees F. Meanwhile, use coconut oil cooking oil spray to coat a casserole dish.

2. Add 1 cup of the uncooked quinoa to the bottom of your casserole dish—layer with the red pepper and diced onion. Place the chicken on top of the vegetables.

3. To prep your sauce, mix the fresh ginger, soy sauce, hoisin sauce, 1 cup of water, and minced garlic. You can use a fork to whisk everything together.

4. Pour your sauce evenly over the chicken breast.

5. Place it in the oven and bake for 45 minutes at 375 degrees F, covered. When done, remove from the oven and add 1 cup of cashew nuts and bake for a further 10 minutes.

6. Set your quinoa casserole aside for around 5-10 minutes to give it time to cool and thicken.

7. To serve, garnish with sesame seeds and/or green onion

Nutritional information: Calories 457, Fat 10g, Protein 37g, Carbs 54g

Korean Turkey Meal Prep Bowls

Prep time: 20 minutes

Cook time: 20 minutes

Total time: 40 minutes

Servings: 4

Ingredients

1 tablespoon of olive oil

3/4 cup of uncooked rice

1 head of broccoli, chopped into florets

Turkey

3/4 lb. of lean ground turkey

4 cloves of minced garlic

1 tablespoon of finely chopped ginger

Sauce

3 tablespoons of honey

3 tablespoons of reduced-sodium soy sauce

1 1/2 teaspoons of sesame oil

1/4 teaspoon of red pepper flakes

1/8 teaspoon of pepper

Garnish

Green onions (optional)

Directions

1. Cook the rice according to the directions on your package. Portion it out into 4 meal prep containers – each having a 2-cup capacity, and allow it to cool.

2. Shake the ingredients for the sauce before setting it aside.

3. In a large pan, heat the oil over medium heat. Add the broccoli and cook for approximately 5 minutes, or until it softens slightly. Remove from the heat and divide it between meal prep containers.

4. Add turkey to the pan and use a spatula to break it up as it cooks. Continue cooking for about 5-8 minutes until no longer pink and completely cooked through.

5. In the middle of the pan, make a space and add the garlic and ginger. Cook for approximately 1 minute as you stir it a bit.

6. Shake up the sauce and pour it over the ginger/garlic and ground turkey. Stir it for about 1-2 minutes until well mixed, then remove it from the heat.

7. Divide the sauce and turkey mixture equally between the meal prep containers. Sprinkle with the green onions if you desire.

Nutritional information: Calories 380, Fat 7g, Protein 28g, Carbs 52g

Recipe notes

1. Once the food has cooled down, store it in the fridge for up to 4 days

2. When you are ready to eat, heat the Korean turkey in the microwave until it is steaming hot

Roasted Brussels Sprout Bowls

Prep time: 15 minutes

Cook time: 40 minutes

Total time: 55 minutes

Servings: 4

Ingredients

Mashed potatoes

1/2 teaspoon of salt

1/2 cup of milk

2.5 lbs. of russet potatoes

2 tablespoon of butter

Creamy Dijon dressing

1 tablespoon of Dijon mustard

1 tablespoon of red wine vinegar

1/4 teaspoon of sugar

Freshly cracked pepper

3 tablespoons of olive oil

1 tablespoon of mayonnaise

1/8 teaspoon of salt

1/16 teaspoon of garlic powder

Roasted brussels sprouts and sausage

1 lb. of fresh Brussels sprouts

2 tablespoons of olive oil

12 oz. of vegetarian Italian sausage

Directions

1. Peel and cube potatoes into 1-inch pieces. Rinse well in a colander and then transfer them to a pot. Add ½ teaspoon of salt and just enough water to cover. Place a lid on the pot, then set heat on high. Heat until the water starts to boil. Boil the potatoes until they are tender enough (approximately 7-10 minutes), drain the potatoes in a colander then rinse them with hot water to remove excess starch.

2. As the potatoes drain, return the pot to the stove and then add milk and butter. Heat on low heat until the milk is hot and the butter melts fully. Return the potatoes you cooked to the pot and turn off the heat. Mash until smooth, then season with pepper and salt to your liking.

3. Meanwhile, in a small jar or bowl, combine all the remaining ingredients (garlic powder, olive oil, red wine vinegar, pepper, salt, garlic powder, sugar, mayonnaise, and Dijon) and whisk them until well combined. Set aside.

4. Preheat your oven to 425 degrees F. Meanwhile, remove any damaged or wilted leaves from the Brussels sprouts and then halve them. Slice the sausages into medallions with a width of 1/2 "

5. To a large baking dish, add the sausage and Brussels sprouts and drizzle with 2 tablespoons of olive oil. Toss the sausage and Brussels Sprouts until everything is fully coated and your baking dish has fairly covered with oil as well. Roast the sausage and Brussels sprouts in the now ready oven for around 20-25 minutes, stirring once (halfway through) until well browned. When done, season with a pinch of salt. Serve by adding 1 cup of mashed potatoes, followed by ¼ of the sausage and Brussels sprouts you roasted, then drizzle a few spoonful of the Dijon dressing you made before serving.

Nutritional information: Calories 638.68, Fat 34.13g, Protein 21.73g, Carbs 69.03g

Steak Cobb Salad Meal Prep

Prep time: 30 minutes

Cook time: 15 minutes

Total time: 45 minutes

Servings: 4

Ingredients

1 pound of steak

Freshly ground black pepper and kosher salt, to taste

6 cups of baby spinach

1 cup Fisher nuts pecan halves

2 tablespoons of unsalted butter

2 tablespoons of olive oil

6 large eggs

1 cup of cherry tomatoes, halved

1/2 cup of crumbled feta cheese

Directions

1. In a large skillet, melt the butter over medium-high heat.

2. Pat both sides of the steak dry using paper towels, then drizzle with the olive oil. Season pepper and salt to taste.

3. Add the steak to the skillet with the melted butter and cook to the desired tenderness. Flip once as you cook (around 3-4 minutes on each side for a medium-rare

steak). Turn off the heat and let it cool before you dice it to bite-sized pieces.

4. In a large saucepan, place the eggs and cover them with cold water by at least 1 inch. Let it boil and cook for at least one minute. Cover the saucepan using a tight-fitting lid, then proceed to remove it from. Set it aside for around 8-10 minutes, then drain well and allow it to cool before you peel and dice.

5. To prepare the salad, place the spinach into meal prep containers and top with rows of eggs, steak, pecans, tomatoes, and feta.

6. Serve with the balsamic vinaigrette or a dressing of your choice. Enjoy!

Nutritional information: Calories 640.3, Fat 51g, Protein 38.8g, Carbs 9.8g

Salsa Chicken Bowls

Prep time: 10 minutes

Cook time: 50 minutes

Total time: 60 minutes

Servings: 4

Ingredients

Brown rice

1/2 a teaspoon of salt

1 cup of brown rice

1.75 cup of water

Salsa chicken

16 oz. of salsa

1 teaspoon of chili powder

2 boneless, skinless chicken breasts

1/2 cup of chicken broth

Roasted bell peppers

1 tablespoon of oil

3 bell peppers

Pinch of salt

Toppings

4 tablespoons of sour cream

2 sliced green onions

Directions

1. Preheat your oven to 425 degrees F. Meanwhile, cook the brown to the instructions on the package. Add the salt, water, and rice to a pot and cover, let it boil over high heat, then turn the heat to low and let it simmer for 35 minutes.

2. As the rice cooks, prepare the chicken. To a medium-sized saucepot, add the chicken breasts along with the chili powder, salsa, and chicken broth. Stir everything briefly.

3. Place a tight-fitting lid on the pot and let it come to a boil over high heat. Once it starts boiling, turn the heat down to low and let the chicken simmer for approximately 30 minutes.

4. As the chicken and rice continue to cook, prepare the bell peppers by slicing them up into ½-wide strips then proceed to placing them on a baking sheet. Next, drizzle with cooking oil and then toss the peppers, making sure that you coat them in oil completely, then sprinkle them with a pinch of salt.

5. In the now hot oven, roast the peppers for around 20-25 minutes or until they turn brown on the edges. Stir once halfway through.

6. After the chicken simmers for 30 minutes, remove it from the salsa mixture and shred the meat using 2 forks. Return the chicken to the salsa pot and stir it well.

7. After your rice has rested, and you have finished shredding the chicken, and your peppers are nicely roasted, now you can build your bowls.

8. To each container, add around ¾ cup of rice, then ¼ of the roasted peppers, followed by a ¼ of the shredded chicken. Spoon some of the salsa from the pot over the chicken. Top with a dollop of sour cream and sliced green onions and serve immediately or store in your fridge for up to 4 days.

Nutritional information: Calories 449.05, Fat 42.4g, Protein 37.7g, Carbs 45.2g

Cashew Chicken Sheet Pan

Prep time: 10 minutes

Cook time: 20 minutes

Total time: 30 minutes

Servings: 4

Ingredients

For the sauce

1 tablespoon of hoisin sauce

2 tablespoons of honey or a low carb sweetener (monk fruit/erythritol/stevia)

½ teaspoon of fresh minced ginger

2 tablespoons of arrowroot starch or cornstarch

6 tablespoons of low sodium-soy sauce coconut aminos

¾ tablespoon of apple cider vinegar

1 teaspoon of toasted sesame oil

2 cloves of minced garlic

½ cup water

For the vegetables and chicken

Black pepper and salt to taste

1 red bell pepper

2/3 cup of unsalted and roasted cashews

2 medium skinless, boneless chicken breasts or thighs, cut into 1"-inch cubes

1 ½ cups of broccoli florets

½ green bell pepper (optional)

Directions

1. Whisk together cornstarch, water, garlic, ginger, honey, sesame oil, vinegar, honey, soy sauce, and hoisin sauce until well combined. Then proceed to bring to a simmer as you stir constantly until the sauce bubbles and thickens. Remove it from the heat and set it aside

For the veggies and chicken

1. Preheat your oven to 400 degrees F. Meanwhile, use a foil that has been coated using parchment paper or cooking spray to line a large parchment paper. Set aside.

2. Season the chicken with black pepper and salt, then drizzle with a few spoonsfuls of sauce to coat the chicken on both sides—Reserve at least half of the sauce to use later.

3. Cook the chicken in the preheated oven for about 8 minutes, then remove the pan.

4. Arrange the cashews, broccoli florets, and bell peppers in one layer around the chicken and season the veggies with peppers and salt. Drizzle a few spoonsful of the sauce on the veggies and toss to coat. Return the chicken to the oven and cook for an extra 8-12

minutes or until the juice run clear and the chicken is cooked through.

5. Remove the pan from the oven and drizzle with the remaining sauce. Serve over your favorite side (maybe cauliflower rice, potatoes, quinoa, or rice) and garnish with sesame seeds and green onions if you desire to. Enjoy!

Nutritional information: Calories 251, Fat 11g, Protein 12g, Carbs 27g

Maple Ginger Chicken Lunch Bowls

Prep time: 15 minutes

Cook time: 25 minutes

Total time: 40 minutes

Servings: 4

Ingredients

Stir fry

2 tablespoons of divided olive oil

2 cloves of minced garlic

2 large chicken breasts/thighs

3/4 cup of uncooked rice of choice

2 tablespoons of finely grated ginger

5 cups of vegetables

Sauce:

5 tablespoons of maple syrup

1/4-1/2 teaspoon of red pepper flakes to taste

3 tablespoons of soy sauce

1 teaspoon of sesame oil

2 teaspoons of cornstarch

Optional

1/4 cup cashews

Directions

1. Cook the rice according to the instructions on the package, then set it aside
2. Shake all the sauce ingredients together and set them aside.

3. Heat 1 tablespoon of oil in a medium wok or pan over medium heat.

4. Add the veggies and let them cook until they are slightly tender (around 5 minutes). When ready, transfer the vegetables to a bowl, then add another tablespoon of oil to the pan.

5. Add the chicken to the pan and let it cook until no longer pink in the middle (approximately 5-7 minutes). Add the ginger and garlic and let it cook for an extra minute.

6. Give the stir fry sauce another good shake and add it to the pan. Let it cook for another minute or until it thickens.

7. Serve by dividing the food amongst four meal prep containers. Spoon some of the extra sauce over the chicken. If using cashews, scatter them over the meal prep containers.

Nutritional information: Calories 463, Fat 12g, Protein 35g, Carbs 54g

Quinoa And Steak Burrito Bowl

Prep time: 20 minutes

Cook time: 20 minutes

Total time: 40 minutes

Servings: 4

Ingredients

16 oz of sirloin steak

1 sliced green pepper

1 avocado

2 tablespoons of divided olive oil

1 sliced red pepper

1 sliced red onion

Quinoa

1/2 cup of quinoa

1 pinch of salt

1 cup of water

1 teaspoon of butter

Corn Salsa

1 can of rinsed and drained black beans

1 teaspoon of hot sauce

1 teaspoon of salt

1 cup of corn

1 tablespoon of lime juice

2 tablespoons of chopped cilantro

1/2 teaspoon of pepper

Pico de Gallo

1 small finely diced onion

2 tablespoons of finely chopped cilantro

2 diced tomatoes

1 tablespoon of lime juice

1 teaspoon of salt

Directions

1. Prepare your quinoa in a pot on the stove or in a rice cooker. Meanwhile, mix the ingredients for the Pico de Gallo and corn salsa together.

2. To a large frying pan, add 1 tablespoon of olive oil and heat over medium-high heat. When the pan starts to smoke, add the steak and cook it for 2-3 minutes per side (depends on the thickness), and on high heat. When the steak is firm enough (not super squishy), take it off the heat. Let it rest for around 5 minutes before you slice it up across the grain. When the steak is ready, keep the frying pan on heat.

3. Add the remaining veggies and 1 tablespoon of olive oil and allow it to sauté for at least 5 minutes, stirring occasionally.

4. To serve in meal prep containers, add the sliced steak, salsas, stir-fried veggies, and sliced avocado around the quinoa. Add your favorite sour cream, hot sauce, salsa, cilantro, and sour cream as garnishes.

Nutritional information: Calories 549, Fat 23g, Protein 37g, Carbs 51g

Hummus Lunch Box

Prep time: 5 minutes

Cook time: 0 minutes

Total time: 5 minutes

Servings: 4

Ingredients

2 pita bread

1 pint of grape tomatoes

1 cucumber

1 cup of hummus

1 6oz. jar of kalamata olives

Directions

1. Cut the pita bread into triangles and slice the cucumber

2. Divide the tomatoes, hummus, olives, cucumber, and pita triangles between 4 meal prep containers.

Nutritional information: Calories 362.55, Fat 22.9g, Protein 8.58g, Carbs 36.28g

Recipe notes

1. Keep refrigerated for up to 5 days.

Egg Roll in a Bowl

Prep time: 10 minutes

Cook time: 15 minutes

Total time: 25 minutes

Servings: 4

Ingredients

1 tablespoon of sesame oil

3 cloves of minced garlic

1/4 cup of liquid soy seasoning

1 tablespoon of monk fruit sweetener (or 2 tablespoons honey or maple syrup)

1 lb. of ground pork

1 tablespoon of finely grated fresh ginger

12 oz of Mann's Broccoli Cole Slaw

2 tablespoons of apple cider vinegar

Optional garnishes

2 tablespoons green onions

1 tablespoon of sesame seeds

Directions

1. Over medium heat, heat a non-stick pan.
2. Add the pork and cook as you break it using a spatula or until no longer pink. Drain any excess grease in the pan.

3. Create a space in the middle of the saucepan and add the garlic ginger and sesame oil—Cook for one minute. Empty the Coleslaw bag onto the pan and cook for 3 more minutes as you stir frequently.

4. As it cooks, shake the apple cider vinegar, soy seasoning, and monk fruit sweetener together and pour evenly into the pan, then toss to coat.

5. Sprinkle with green onions, and sesame seeds (optional) enjoy!

Nutritional information: Calories 320, Fat 28g, Protein 23g, Carbs 9g

Recipe notes

1. To store, portion out in storage containers with a 2-cup capacity and store in the fridge for up to 4 days.

2. This recipe can either be eaten cold or heated through.

Chicken Salad with Creamy No-Mayo Dressing

Prep time: 10 minutes

Cook time: 15 minutes

Total time: 25 minutes

Servings: 4

Ingredients

Salads:

3 ribs of chopped celery

2 teaspoons of lemon juice

8 leaves chopped romaine lettuce

2 skinless chicken half breasts, boneless

1 chopped apple

1 cup of halved grapes

½ cup of toasted pecans

Dressing:

1 1/2 tablespoons of apple cider vinegar

1 tablespoon of lemon juice

1 teaspoon of poppy seeds

¾ cup of Greek yogurt

1 tablespoon of honey

2 tablespoons of water

Pepper and salt

Directions

1. Over medium heat, heat a large or medium skillet and spray it using a cooking spray. Add the chicken and season it with pepper and salt. Cook for 2-3 minutes, or until it browns on one side, then flip and cook the other side for 2 more minutes.

2. Add water such that it reaches halfway up the side of the chicken. Cover your skillet with a fitting lid. Continue cooking until cooked through. Remove the chicken and place it on a plate to cool.

3. Meanwhile, prepare your salads by whisking all the dressing ingredients together. Taste and add more honey (1/2 a teaspoon) if need be. Divide the dressing into 4 (16-ounce) mason jars equally. Toss the pieces of apple with 2 teaspoons of lemon juice.

4. Once your chicken is cool enough, chop it into bite-sized pieces

5. Divide the remaining ingredient equally between the 4 mason jars in this order; celery followed by chicken, then apples and then grapes, follow it with lettuce and finally pecans. Next, seal the jars and store them in the refrigerator for up to 3 days. When you are ready to

eat, just give the jar a good shake and pour the salad onto a plate or bowl.

Nutritional information: Calories 287, Fat 12g, Protein 24g, Carbs 23g

Recipe notes

1. If you want more lettuce in your salad, then use 32-ounce mason jars.

The Pizza Roll-Up Lunch Box

Prep time: 15 minutes

Cook time: 0 minutes

Total time: 15 minutes

Servings: 4

Ingredients

1/4 cup of basil pesto

36 slices of pepperoni

1/2 cup of pizza sauce

4 large burrito sized tortillas

8 slices of provolone cheese

4 cups of fresh spinach

2 green bell peppers

Directions

1. Spread 1 tablespoon of pesto over on the surface of the tortillas (you don't need to cover the whole surface). Lay 2 slices of provolone on each half of the tortillas, followed by 9 pepperonis. Add some spinach (a handful of fresh ones) to every tortilla.

2. Roll up each of the tortillas, ensuring that you keep the roll as tight as possible. Turn it such that the seams are facing downwards, then slice the rolls into 1-inch sections. Place the sliced rolls in your meal prep containers, ensuring that you pack them as close together as possible to prevent them from unwrapping.

3. Slice your green peppers into strips and divide the strips equally between the meal prep containers.

4. Fill up four small containers, each with 2 tablespoons of pizza sauce. Store your pizza sauce, roll-ups, and pizza sauce in the refrigerator for up to 5 days.

Nutritional information: Calories 598, Fat 35.1g, Protein 26.3g, Carbs 44.2g

Tuna Salad

Prep time: 20 minutes

Cook time: 0 minutes

Total time: 20 minutes

Servings: 4

Ingredients

Classic tuna salad

2 12 oz. cans of chunk light tuna in water

1/4 cup of chopped walnuts

1/2 cup of mayonnaise

1/4 teaspoon of salt

1 cup of diced celery

2 sliced green onions

1 tablespoon of lemon juice

1/4 teaspoon of freshly cracked black pepper

Other ingredients

12 mini sweet peppers

4 ribs of celery

20 crackers

Directions

1. Drain your tuna well. Slice the green onion and dice the celery. Combine the pepper, salt, lemon juice, mayonnaise, walnuts, green onion, tuna, and celery in a bowl. Stir until evenly combined.

2. Next, slice any remaining celery nicely to form sticks, then proceed to cut each of the sweet peppers into halves and remove out the seeds.

3. Divide the tuna salad between 4 containers (around 1 cup each). Add the crackers, mini sweet peppers,

celery sticks, and crackers to each box with tuna salad. For an extra layer of protection, pack them separately or wrap each of the crackers in a sandwich baggie. Refrigerate for up to 4 days

Nutritional information: Calories 573.98, Fat 34.8g, Protein 44.1g, Carbs 18.93g

Cold Sesame Noodles Made With Spiralized Vegetables

Prep time: 20 minutes

Cook time: 10 minutes

Total time: 30 minutes

Servings: 4

Ingredients

4 oz of uncooked whole-wheat spaghetti

1 spiralized medium-sized zucchini

2 large shredded or spiralized carrots

Sesame seeds and green onions to garnish

2 cups of drained & rinsed chickpeas

Almond Butter Sauce:

1/4 cup of almond butter

1 clove of minced garlic

3 tablespoons of rice vinegar

1 tablespoon of maple syrup

1 teaspoon of finely grated ginger

2 tablespoons of soy sauce

1 tablespoon of sesame oil

1 teaspoon of lime juice

1/2 teaspoon of red pepper flakes (omit for non-spicy version)

Directions

1. Cook the pasta according to the instructions on the package. Rinse using cold water and set it aside to cool down completely.

2. Portion out the zoodles, pasta, chickpeas, and carrot noodles between 4 2-cup storage containers. Sprinkle with sesame seeds and green onions.

3. Shake together or stir together all the ingredients for the butter sauce and divide it equally amongst 2 oz storage containers.

Nutritional information: Calories 452, Fat 15g, Protein 19g, Carbs 65g

Recipe notes

1. To store, keep in the fridge for up to 4 days. This recipe is not freezer friendly.

2. Enjoy while cold. Drizzle with the almond butter sauce and toss before serving.

3. You can swap almond butter with natural peanut butter.

Smoky Roasted Sausage And Vegetables

Prep time: 15 minutes

Cook time: 40 minutes

Total time: 55 minutes

Servings: 4

Ingredients

Smoky vinaigrette

2 tablespoon of red wine vinegar

1/4 teaspoon of garlic powder

1/2 teaspoon of smoked paprika

Freshly cracked black pepper

1/4 cup of olive oil

1 teaspoon of dijon or coarse deli mustard

1/4 teaspoon of dried oregano

1/4 teaspoon of salt

1/4 teaspoon of sugar

Veggies and sausage

12 oz. of smoked sausage

1 bell pepper (any color)

1 lb. of broccoli crown

1 red onion

For serving

1 handful of chopped parsley

1 cup of uncooked long-grain white rice

Directions

1. Preheat your oven to 400 degrees F. Meanwhile, use parchment paper to line a large baking sheet.

2. Combine the vinaigrette ingredients in a jar or small bowl and whisk thoroughly or if using a jar, close the lid and shake thoroughly until well combined. Set it aside. Slice up the smoked sausages to ½ inch medallions, then cut the broccoli into small florets. Dice the onion and bell pepper into 1- inch pieces. Place the onion, broccoli, sausage, and bell pepper onto the baking sheet.

3. Drizzle 2 tablespoons of vinaigrette onto the veggies and sausage and toss to coat.

4. Roast for approximately 35-40 minutes, stirring once halfway through until the edges start to brown. As the veggies and sausage continue roasting, cook the rice.

5. To a saucepot, add 2 cups of water and the rice. Place a lid on the pot and let it come to a boil over high heat. When it boils, turn the heat to low and allow it to simmer for 15 minutes. Turn off the heat and let it

rest, with the lid still in place, for 5 more minutes. Before serving, fluff with a fork.

6. When the veggies and sausage are ready, add the remaining half of the vinaigrette and toss to coat. If need be, season with an extra pinch of pepper and salt.

7. To serve, add ¾ cup of rice to each meal prep bowl along with ¼ of the roasted veggies and sausage. Drizzle another spoonful of vinaigrette over the top and sprinkle some fresh parsley to finish.

Nutritional information: Calories 660, Fat 42.8g, Protein 17.6g, Carbs 50.2g

Sheet Pan ginger, Garlic Chicken and Broccoli

Prep time: 15 minutes

Cook time: 15 minutes

Total time: 30 minutes

Servings: 4

Ingredients

Garlic Ginger Sauce

3/4 cup of low sodium soy sauce

1/2 cup of water

1/4 cup of white vinegar

1/4 cup of olive oil

2-inch knob of freshly peeled ginger

4 cloves of garlic

¼ cup of sugar/honey or 4 Medjool dates

Broccoli and chicken

1 pound of boneless skinless chicken thighs or breasts, cut into strips

1 head of broccoli, cut into florets

1 red pepper, cut into strips

green onions, sesame seeds, sesame oil, for topping

Directions

1. To prepare the sauce, preheat your oven to 425 degrees F and blend all the ingredients for the sauce

together until smooth. Place the red pepper, broccoli, and chicken on a sheet pan. Pour ½ a cup of sauce over the chicken and a couple of tablespoons over the vegetables. Bake for approximately 10-15 minutes.

2. As the chicken and broccoli roasts, simmer another ½ cup of sauce over medium-low heat in a small saucepan until it thickens. Drizzle it over the broccoli and chicken. Top with blend scallions, sesame seeds, or sesame oil.

Nutritional information: Calories 409, Fat 17.7g, Protein 34.1g, Carbs 31.9g

Recipe notes

1. If you have some extra sauce after cooking, save it for use next time.

2. Store in the fridge for up to 4 days.

3. For a vegetarian version, substitute chicken with tofu.

4. If you prefer dry and crispy broccoli, cook it on a different baking sheet.

Buddha Bowl

Prep time: 15 minutes

Cook time: 25 minutes

Total time: 40 minutes

Servings: 4

Ingredients

Chickpea Buddha Bowls

2 large carrots, peeled & chopped

2 cups of brussels sprouts (outer leaves removed and cut in half)

Pepper and salt

3/4 cup of uncooked quinoa

1 red onion chopped into 1-inch pieces

2 tablespoons of olive oil

19 oz can of chickpeas (drained)

Tahini Dressing

2 tablespoons of water

2 teaspoons of lemon juice

2 tablespoons of tahini

2 teaspoons of maple syrup

Salt

Directions

1. Cook the quinoa according to the directions on the package. Divide it equally into four 2-cup capacity storage containers and let It cool.

2. Heat your oven to 435 degrees F and use parchment paper to line a baking sheet. Set it aside.

3. Toss the onion, carrots, and brussels sprouts in olive oil and then season with pepper and salt.

4. Spread out on the baking sheet you prepared, then bake in the oven for about 15-20 minutes until the veggies soften. Stir halfway through the cooking period.

5. As the veggies bake, shake the tahini dressing ingredients together.

6. Set out four meal prep containers and portion out the veggies, chickpeas, and tahini sauce equally. Enjoy!

Nutritional information: Calories 496, Fat 16g, Protein 19g, Carbs 70g

Recipe notes

1. You can store it in the fridge for up to 4 days. When ready to eat, just reheat until steaming hot or enjoy it cold.

Honey Sesame Chicken Bowls

Prep time: 10 minutes

Cook time: 20 minutes

Total time: 30 minutes

Servings: 4

Ingredients

Honey Sesame Sauce

1/4 cup of reduced-sodium soy sauce

1 tablespoon of sesame oil

1 teaspoon of cornstarch

1/4 cup of water or chicken stock

1/4 cup of maple syrup or honey

1/2 teaspoon of red pepper flakes

Chicken Lunch Bowls

2 tablespoons of divided olive oil

3 cups of snap peas (with ends trimmed)

Salt & pepper

3/4 cup of uncooked rice (or 2 cups cooked)

3 cups of broccoli (chopped into small pieces)

2 large chicken breasts (cut into 1-inch cubes)

Sesame seeds (for garnishing)

Directions

1. Shake all the honey sesame sauce ingredients together and set them aside.

2. Cook the rice according to the instructions on the package. When ready, divide it equally between 4 storage containers.

3. In a large pan, heat 1 tablespoon of olive oil. Add the snap peas and broccoli. Cook for about 5-7 minutes or until tender and bright green. When ready, add to the storage containers with the rice.

4. Add 1 tablespoon of olive oil to the pan, then add the chicken. Season with pepper and salt, then add the red pepper flakes (if you would like to). Continue cooking -until cooked through (approximately 7-10 minutes).

5. Add the sauce to the pan and let it simmer until it thickens (approximately 2 minutes.)

6. Then add the chicken to the storage containers before drizzling with sauce.

7. Finally, garnish with the sesame seeds if you'd like to. Store in your refrigerator for up to 4 days. Reheat when ready to eat. Enjoy!

Nutritional information: Calories 483.19, Fat 14.29g, Protein 31.74g, Carbs 57.74g

Recipe notes

1. If you would like to lighten this recipe, then try replacing the rice with cauliflower rice or reducing the sauce by half.

Honey Sriracha Glazed Meatballs

Prep time: 5 minutes

Cook time: 25 minutes

Total time: 30 minutes

Servings: 8

Ingredients

For the meatballs:

1 cup of whole-wheat panko breadcrumbs

1/4 cup of chopped green onions

1/2 teaspoon of salt

2 lb. of lean ground turkey

2 eggs

1/2 teaspoon of garlic powder

1/2 teaspoon of black pepper

For the sauce:

1/4 cup of Sriracha

3 tablespoons of rice vinegar

1 tablespoon of freshly grated ginger

1/2 teaspoon of toasted sesame oil

3 Tablespoon of reduced-sodium soy sauce

3 tablespoons of honey

3 cloves of minced garlic

Directions

1. Preheat your oven to 375 degrees F. Mix together the breadcrumbs, turkey, salt, pepper, and green onions until well combined. Shape the mixture into 1 ½" balls and place them on a baking sheet spaced apart and spray lightly using a cooking spray.

2. Bake the meatballs for 20-25 minutes until cooked through or browned. Meanwhile, in a small saucepan, combine all the sauce ingredients and boil over medium heat. Whisk continuously. Reduce the heat and let it simmer until the sauce starts to thicken around 8-10 minutes. Toss in the meatballs.

3. Serve immediately with brown rice and top with a few sesame seeds and green onions.

Nutritional information: Calories 296, Fat 10.8g, Protein 26.9g, Carbs 18.7g

Cheesy Chicken and Rice

Prep time: 20 minutes

Cook time: 20 minutes

Total time: 40 minutes

Servings: 4

Ingredients

2 tablespoons of olive oil

1 crown of broccoli (or 4 cups of bite-sized pieces)

1/2 head of cauliflower

Salt and pepper

1 cup of shredded mozzarella cheese

Chicken

1 tablespoon of olive oil

1 teaspoon of onion powder

1/4 teaspoon of pepper

1 lb. of boneless skinless chicken breasts (cut into bite-sized pieces)

1 teaspoon of garlic powder

1/4 teaspoon of salt

Directions

1. Make cauliflower by cutting the cauliflower into even-sized pieces. In a food processor, pulse the cauliflower until it breaks down to cauliflower rice (10-15 times). You can also use a box grater to make the cauliflower rice.

2. To a non-stick pan, add 1 tablespoon of olive oil and heat over medium heat. Add the cauliflower rice and allow it to cook for about 5 minutes or until it softens slightly. Season with pepper and salt. Divide between 4 2-cup capacity storage containers.

3. Add another tablespoon of olive oil to the pan and add the broccoli. Cook it until it softens slightly (around 5-7 minutes). Add the broccoli to the storage containers.

4. To cook the chicken, toss it together with pepper, salt, olive oil, garlic powder, and onion powder. Use a non-stick pan to cook over medium heat for around 5-7 minutes, or until cooked through. Add the chicken to the storage containers.

5. Divide the shredded cheese into the storage containers and store it in the fridge for up to 4 days. When ready to eat, microwave it until steaming hot. Stir and enjoy.

Nutritional information: Calories 329, Fat 19g, Protein 31g, Carbs 5g

Snacks Recipes

Homemade Beef Jerky Recipe

Prep time: 10 minutes

Cook time: 5 hours

Freezing & marinating time: 1hour 30minutes

Servings: 8

Ingredients

16 oz of top sirloin steak

1/4 cup of Worcestershire sauce

2 teaspoons of hot sauce

1 teaspoon of onion powder

1 teaspoon of paprika

3/4 cup of low sodium soy sauce

2 tablespoons of honey

2 teaspoons of black pepper

1 teaspoon of garlic powder

1/2 teaspoon of red pepper flakes

Directions

1. Freeze the steak for about 1 hour, then slice it thinly against the grain. Ensure to trim away all fat.

2. Mix the marinade ingredients together, then add to a large freezer bag. Add the strips of steak to the bag and allow them to marinate for at least 30 minutes

3. Preheat your oven to 170 degrees F, then place the strips of steak on a plate lined with a paper towel. Squeeze out the excess liquid from the strips using a paper towel until fully dried. Add the steak strips to skewers, then hang them on the highest rack in your oven.

4. Close the door of your oven and prop it open slightly using an oven mitt. This allows moisture to escape— Cook for 5 hours. When done, remove the jerky from the skewers and keep them in the fridge for up to 14 days.

Nutritional information: Calories 108, Fat 2g, Protein 14g, Carbs 8g

Quinoa Peanut Butter Cup Protein Balls

Prep time: 10 minutes

Cook time: 0 minutes

Total time: 10 minutes

Servings: 15

Ingredients

1 cup of cooked quinoa

1/2 cup of peanut butter

1/4 cup of chocolate chips (dairy-free/vegan if necessary)

1/4 cup of chia seeds

1 teaspoon of vanilla

Directions

1. Stir together all the ingredients above, excluding the chocolate chips.

2. Use a spoon to scoop the mixture and roll it into balls. Place the balls on parchment paper to set.

3. Melt the chocolate chips in a microwave-safe dish. Microwave at intervals of 30 seconds as you stir in between until smooth. Drizzle the chocolate over the quinoa balls.

4. Place the balls in your fridge to set. Once they harden, transfer them to an airtight container and store them in your fridge.

Nutritional information: Calories 103, Fat 6.8g, Protein 3.3g, Carbs 8.4g

Peanut Butter Bites

Prep time: 10 minutes

Cook time: 0 minutes

Total time: 10 minutes

Servings: 18

Ingredients

2 tablespoons of unsweetened cocoa powder

2 tablespoons of agave

1/2 cup of protein powder

1 cup of water

1 1/2 cups of rolled oats

2 tablespoon of ground flax

1/2 cup of peanut butter

1/4 cup of chia Seeds

Directions

1. Combine the protein powder, water, and chia seeds in a medium-sized bowl. Set the mixture in your fridge for 5 minutes until It turns to a gel.

2. Meanwhile, combine the rest of the ingredients in a larger separate bowl. Add the gel to the bowl and stir well to combine.

3. Use your hands to roll the batter you just made into balls. Wet your hands constantly to make the process easier.

4. In a container, place the balls in your fridge and let them sit for 20 minutes, then enjoy!

Nutritional information: Calories 117, Fat 6g, Protein 8g, Carbs 10g

Recipe notes

1. You can store these balls in the fridge for up to one week or in the freezer for up to 1 month.

No-Bake Pb & J Energy Bites

Prep time: 15 minutes

Cook time: 0 minutes

Total time: 15 minutes

Servings: 14

Ingredients

1/2 cup of creamy salted peanut butter (or cashew, or almond, or sun butter)

2 tablespoons of vegan protein powder (optional)

2 1/2 tablespoons of flaxseed meal

1/4 cup of dried fruit (dried strawberries, blueberries, cherries, cranberries)

1/4 cup of maple syrup (finely chopped dates)

1 1/4 cup of gluten-free rolled oats

2 tablespoons of chia seeds

Directions

1. Add protein powder, peanut butter, rolled oats, maple syrup, dried fruit, chia seeds, and flaxseed meal to a large mixing bowl. Mix thoroughly until well combined. If too crumbly/dry, add more maple syrup or peanut butter. If it is too wet or sticky, add some more flaxseed meal or oats.

2. Chill in your fridge for about 5 minutes, then scoop out approximately 1 ½ tablespoon amounts and roll into balls.

3. Enjoy immediately.

Nutritional information: Calories 117, Fat 1.71g, Protein 3.6g, Carbs 13.8g

Recipe notes

1. Store in the refrigerator for 1 week or in the freezer for 1 month.

2. For gluten-free, you should substitute the oats with shredded unsweetened coconut, chopped nuts, and more dried fruit.

Protein Brownie Bites

Prep time: 5 minutes

Cook time: 15 minutes

Total time: 20 minutes

Servings: 12

Ingredients

1 cup of pumpkin puree

1/4 cup of cocoa powder

1 serving of liquid stevia

1/2 cup of almond butter

1-2 scoops of protein powder

Directions

1. Preheat your oven to 350 degrees F. Meanwhile, line your muffin tin with mini muffin liners. For smaller brownie bites, you will require at least 15. Make sure you grease each muffin tin generously.

2. Combine all your ingredients in a mixing bowl or high-speed blender and mix/blend until smooth.

3. Pour the mixture into each muffin tin until just full since they won't be rising.

4. Bake for around 12-15 minutes, or until a toothpick or skewer comes out just clean. Remove from the oven and allow it to cool completely. For the best result, after cooling, keep in the fridge for a few hours.

Nutritional information: Calories 95, Fat 4g, Protein 8g, Carbs 5g

Recipe notes

1. Keep the brownie bites refrigerated for the best taste

2. If you prefer mixing by hand, then you might have some banana chunks

3. Since the brownie bites do not have eggs, if you want them to be ultra-fudgy, then you should remove them from the oven earlier

Healthy Chocolate Raspberry Protein Bars

Prep time: 15 minutes

Cook time: 0 minutes

Total time: 15 minutes

Servings: 16

Ingredients

1 cup of brown rice flour

1/4 cup of unsweetened almond milk

1/4 cup + 2 tablespoons of sugar-free maple syrup

3 tablespoons of sugar-free chocolate chips

1/2 cup of freeze-dried raspberries

32g of vanilla protein powder

1/4 cup of cashew butter or any nut butter of choice

2 tablespoons of granulated zero-calorie sweetener

Directions

1. Use a blender or food processor to process the freeze-dried raspberries on high until in powder form.

2. Pour the powder, flour, protein, and sweetener into a mixer. Mix until well combined. Add in the almond milk, sugar-free maple syrup, cashew butter, and almond milk. Continue mixing until a dough is formed.

3. Line an 8x8 inch pan with parchment paper and press the dough you made evenly into the bottom. Melt the chocolate and drizzle it over the dough. Put the pan into the freezer for around 30 minutes before you cut it into 16 bars. Serve and enjoy!

Nutritional information: Calories 106, Fat 5g, Protein 4g, Carbs 11g

Apple Pie Protein Bars

Prep time: 5 minutes

Cook time: 5 minutes

Total time: 10 minutes

Servings: 12

Ingredients

1 cup of coconut flour

½ cup of protein powder of choice

1 tablespoon of cinnamon

1 teaspoon of nutmeg

½ cup of keto maple syrup

1 tablespoon of milk of choice

½ cup of almond flour

2 tablespoons of granulated sweetener of choice

1 teaspoon of mixed spice

1/4 cup of almond butter (or any nut or seed butter of choice)

1/2 cup of unsweetened applesauce

Directions

1. Use greased paper to line a large baking dish and set it aside.

2. Combine the protein powder, flour, cinnamon, granulated sweetener, mixed spice, and nutmeg well.

3. Combine the liquid sweetener and nut butter in a microwave-safe bowl and heat until melted. Pour the mixture into the dry mixture and add the unsweetened applesauce. Mix until well combined. Use a spoon to add the milk, one spoonful at a time. Continue doing this until a firm batter is formed.

4. Transfer the batter to a baking dish and press it down firmly. Keep in the fridge for 30 minutes. Serve and enjoy!

Nutritional information: Calories 142, Fat 10g, Protein 12g, Carbs 6g

Recipe notes

4. If the batter is too thin, add more coconut flour until firmer.

5. Store the protein bars in the fridge for up to 2 weeks or in the freezer for up to 6 months.

Sweet Pumpkin Protein Granola

Prep time: 10 minutes

Cook time: 30 minutes

Total time: 40 minutes

Servings: 10-14

Ingredients

½ cup of whole wheat flour

¼ cup of chia seeds

⅔ cup of buckwheat groats

Pinch of salt

½ cup of maple syrup

⅔ cup of pumpkin seeds

¼ cup of melted coconut oil

3 cups of rolled oats

½ cup of unsweetened, dried flake coconut

½ teaspoon of cinnamon

1 cup of cooked split red lentils (or ½ cup of dry split red lentils)

¼ cup of coconut palm sugar

Directions

For the granola

1. Preheat your oven to 375 degrees F. Meanwhile, cook the lentils as shown below.

2. Combine the pumpkin seeds, flour, salt, coconut sugar, buckwheat groats, coconut, chia seeds, salt, cinnamon, and oats.

3. Add the cooked red lentils, melted coconut, coconut sugar, and maple syrup. Mix thoroughly. Use parchment paper to line a baking sheet and spread the granola into an even layer over the whole surface.

4. Place in the oven and bake for 8 minutes. Remove from the oven and let it cool for around 5-10 minutes (the longer the granola cools, the more it will have clusters at the end). Once cool, mix and break it up before you redistribute it evenly.

5. Bake for 6 more minutes, then remove from the oven and allow it cool for an extra 5-10 minutes. Once cool, mix and break it up before you redistribute it evenly.

6. Bake for 4-5 more minutes or until the granola is toasted evenly but not burnt. Ensure that you keep a keen eye on the granola as it tends to burn rapidly and suddenly. Cool completely before you break it into clusters. Store in an airtight container.

For the lentils

7. Rinse ½ a cup of dry, split red lentils. To a medium saucepan, add 1 cup of unsalted water and the lentils. Set on the stove and bring to boil for 5-10 minutes, or until the lentils are just tender.

Nutritional information: Calories 335, Fat 11.7g, Protein 10.9g, Carbs 50g

Recipe notes

1. If you prefer it sweeter, then you should use sweetened non-dairy milk, add coconut palm syrup or a dash of maple syrup to each bowl or add dried fruit onto the granola after it cools.

Chocolate Chip Raspberry Crispy Granola Bars

Prep time: 10 minutes

Cook time: 0 minutes

Total time: 10 minutes

Servings: 8

Ingredients

1 1/2 cups of oats

1/3 cup of nut butter of choice

32g of vanilla protein powder

1 tablespoon of mini chocolate chips

1/2 cup of brown rice cereal Erewhon

1/3 cup + 2 tablespoons of all-natural sugar-free maple syrup

1/4 cups of freeze-dried raspberries

Directions

1. Use parchment paper to line an 8x8 inch pan.

2. Warm the maple syrup and nut butter gently in a microwave-safe bowl for 10 seconds. Stir until smooth.

3. Stir together the protein powder, cereal, and oats in a large bowl, and then add the nut syrup/butter stir until you coat the dry ingredients.

4. Fold in the freeze-dried raspberries and chocolate chips.

5. Press and mix evenly into the pan you prepared and keep in the fridge for at least 2 hours. Cut into 8 bars and serve.

Nutritional information: Calories 144, Fat 6.4g, Protein 7.7g, Carbs 14.5g

Carrot Cake Power Bites

Servings: 24

Ingredients

For the power bites:

4 medium peeled carrots, sliced into 1/2-inch pieces

1/2 cup of unsalted creamy almond butter

1/4 teaspoon of ground nutmeg

1 1/2 cups of almond meal, divided

1/2 cup of coarsely chopped & pitted Medjool dates

1 teaspoon of ground cinnamon

1/2 teaspoon of salt

For the icing:

1/4 cup of powdered sugar

1/8 teaspoon of vanilla bean paste or ground vanilla beans, or 1/2 teaspoon vanilla extract

3/4 teaspoon of water

Directions

1. In a medium saucepan, place the carrots then cover them with at least 1 inch of water. Bring it to boil over medium heat, then turn the heat down to low. Simmer for 10 minutes, or until the carrots are fork-tender but not falling apart. Drain in a colander, then set them aside to cool.

2. In a food processor bowl that is fitted with the blade attachment, place the now cool carrots, salt, nutmeg, cinnamon, almond butter, and dates. Process in pulses of 1-second intervals until the dates are fully processed and blended into the dough. Scrape down the sides of the bowl if need be. Transfer to a medium-sized bowl.

3. Add ¾ cup of almond meal. Use a fitted spatula or sturdy spoon to mix until just combined. Refrigerate overnight or for at least 2 hours, until set.

4. When you are ready to roll the bites, make the icing. Start by placing the vanilla, water, and powdered sugar into a small bowl and stirring until all powdered sugar is absorbed to form a thick and pasty icing. Transfer it to a resealable sandwich bag. Squeeze out as much air as possible and seal the bag.

5. Use parchment or wax paper to line a rimmed baking sheet. To a small bowl, add the remaining ¾ cup of almond flour. Use a sturdy spoon to scoop out a heaping tablespoon of chilled dough. Scape the dough of the sides of the first spoon using another spoon. Repeat this until you form a ball shape.

6. Drop the shaped dough into the almond flour and coat completely. Pick it up, and then roll it gently into a ball using your hands. Place it on the baking sheet.

7. Once you roll all the dough into power bites, drizzle with icing (you can snip off a tiny corner of the bag and squeeze to dispense thin squiggles of icing).

Nutritional information: Calories 275, Fat 19.3g, Protein 8.4g, Carbs 21.4g

Recipe notes

2. Store in the fridge. You can pack the power bites in single layers with sheets of parchment paper or wax in between. You can also freeze while still on the baking sheet, then transfer to a freezer container once they solidify.

3. You can keep these bites in the fridge for 3-5 days or in the freezer for 1 month.

Vanilla Cashew Butter Cups

Prep time: 15 minutes

Cook time: 0 minutes

Total time: 15 minutes

Servings: small -24, Large- 12

Ingredients

7 ounces of chocolate chips or chopped dark chocolate

2 tablespoons of honey (or maple syrup)

A pinch of sea salt

1 cup of cashew butter

1 tablespoon of vanilla

Flaky sea salt

Directions

1. Line a 24-cup mini muffin tin or 12 cup muffin tin with liners.

2. In a pan, place 2/3rds of the chocolate chips over low heat. Once mostly melted and has a glossy look, remove from the heat and add the remaining chocolate. Stir a couple of times to allow the remaining heat to melt the chocolate you added.

3. Add less than a teaspoon of the chocolate you melted to a cupcake liner before tipping it on to the side slightly. Next, rotate it such that the chocolate comes 1/3 of the way up the side of the liner. Repeat for the other liners, then place them in the fridge to harden.

4. To a medium-sized bowl, add the salt, vanilla, honey, and cashew butter and fold them gently together. Once the chocolate cups harden, divide the cashew

butter equally between the cups. Press down into cups using your finger.

5. Over the tops of the cashew butter cups, pour the chocolate that remained and then return to the fridge to harden.

6. Sprinkle a little of the flaky salt over the buttercups and enjoy!

Nutritional information: Calories 117, Fat 8.4g, Protein 2.4g, Carbs 8.8g

Recipe notes

1. If you follow the vegan or paleo diet, you should read the label on your chocolate to ensure that it is okay for you to eat.

2. You can melt the chocolate in a microwave for 20-30 seconds

3. You can make your own cashew butter at home using a high-powered blender or food processor. Just add 1 tablespoon of coconut oil and 2 cups of raw cashews and process to make 1 cup of cashew butter.

14 Day Meal Plan

Week 1 Meal Plan

Day 1

Recommended Breakfast

Egg and Sausage McMuffin

Recommended Lunch

Cheesy Chicken and Rice

Recommended Dinner

Cashew Chicken Sheet Pan

Recommended Snack

Vanilla Cashew Butter Cups

Day 2

Recommended Breakfast

Simple Toast With Avocado And Poached Egg

Recommended Lunch

Honey Sriracha Glazed Meatballs

Recommended Dinner

Salsa Chicken Bowls

Recommended Snack

Carrot Cake Power Bites

Day 3

Recommended Breakfast

Protein-Packed Breakfast Burritos

Recommended Lunch

Honey Sesame Chicken Bowls

Recommended Dinner

Steak Cobb Salad Meal Prep

Recommended Snack

Chocolate Chip Raspberry Crispy Granola Bars

Day 4

Recommended Breakfast

Tex Mex Breakfast Quesadillas

Recommended Lunch

Buddha Bowl

Recommended Dinner

Roasted Brussels Sprout Bowls

Recommended Snack

Sweet Pumpkin Protein Granola

Day 5

Recommended Breakfast

Peanut Butter Protein Pancakes

Recommended Lunch

Sheet Pan ginger, Garlic Chicken and Broccoli

Recommended Dinner

Korean Turkey Meal Prep Bowls

Recommended Snack

Apple Pie Protein Bars

Day 6

Recommended Breakfast

Bacon-Wrapped Egg Cups

Recommended Lunch

Smoky Roasted Sausage And Vegetables

Recommended Dinner

Healthy Cashew Chicken Casserole

Recommended Snack

Healthy Chocolate Raspberry Protein Bars

Day 7

Recommended Breakfast

Egg Muffins with Cauliflower Rice, Ham, and Kale

Recommended Lunch

Cold Sesame Noodles Made With Spiralized Vegetables

Recommended Dinner

Spicy Chicken and Sweet Potato

Recommended Snack

Protein Brownie Bites

Week Two Meal Plan

Day 8

Recommended Breakfast

High Protein Salmon Toast

Recommended Lunch

Tuna Salad

Recommended Dinner

Chicken And Avocado Burritos

Recommended Snack

No-Bake Pb & J Energy Bites

Day 9

Recommended Breakfast

Sweet Potato Breakfast Bowls

Recommended Lunch

The Pizza Roll-Up Lunch Box

Recommended Dinner

General Tso's Chickpeas

Recommended Snack

Peanut Butter Bites

Day 10

Recommended Breakfast

Banana Egg Pancakes

Recommended Lunch

Chicken Salad with Creamy No-Mayo Dressing

Recommended Dinner

Kung Pao Chicken

Recommended Snack

Quinoa Peanut Butter Cup Protein Balls

Day 11

Recommended Breakfast

Crockpot Breakfast Casserole

Recommended Lunch

Egg Roll in a Bowl

Recommended Dinner

Creamy Spinach Chicken with Zucchini Noodles

Recommended Snack

Vanilla Cashew Butter Cups

Day 12

Recommended Breakfast

Breakfast Taco Scramble

Recommended Lunch

Hummus Lunch Box

Recommended Dinner

Jerk Chicken Bowls

Recommended Snack

Chocolate Chip Raspberry Crispy Granola Bars

Day 13

Recommended Breakfast

Pina Colada Instant Pot Steel Cut Oats

Recommended Lunch

Quinoa And Steak Burrito Bowl

Recommended Dinner

Greek Marinated Chicken

Recommended Snack

Sweet Pumpkin Protein Granola

Day 14

Recommended Breakfast

Vegetable Egg White Frittata

Recommended Lunch

Maple Ginger Chicken Lunch Bowls

Recommended Dinner

Light Mongolian Beef

Recommended Snack

Healthy Chocolate Raspberry Protein Bars

Conclusion

I hope the book has taught you exactly how you can meal prep and succeed in your journey to building a well-chiseled and built body that you've always desired! All you need to do now is to follow what you have learned to transform your dreams into reality.

Printed in Great Britain
by Amazon